LESSONS LEARNED FROM TALKING TO THE DEAD

D1506329

ROB GUTRO

Photo: Orb Outside of the Thomas Wolfe House, Asheville, N.C.

COVER PHOTO

The cover photo shows an orb outside of the Thomas Wolfe House in Asheville, North Carolina. I took this photo using a digital camera on a night-time ghost walk in October 2010. The orb showed up in one of many photos taken of the outside of the house. The window of the room behind it is where Thomas Wolfe's brother is often seen. Wolfe's brother passed away at a young age and is reputed to still haunt the house.

"Lessons Learned From Talking to the Dead," by Rob Gutro.
ISBN 978-1475033212

DEDICATION

This book is dedicated to my friend Sarah, who passed away during the writing of this book. She loved dogs and even came back to let us and our dogs know that she was at peace on the other side with her beloved dog Shadow.

It is also dedicated to Ed G. who passed in 1996. Ed took us on an incredible journey that joined the afterlife with life on Earth and provided me with so many personal and unique signs that we were able to bring his dad peace after 15 long years of grieving.

CONTENTS

CHAPTER 14: MESSAGES FROM FAMILY MEMBERS (CONT).

CHAPTER 15: SPIRITS USE OF ELECTRICITY AND WATER ENERGY

CHAPTER 16: LOCATIONS AND GHOST INVESTIGATIONS

LESSONS LEARNED FROM TALKING TO THE DEAD

FOREWARD

My name is Rob, and I consider myself an average, middle-aged guy. I'm a scientist (meteorologist) by trade, but since I was a teenager, I've had the ability to see, sense and communicate with Earth-bound ghosts and spirits. Basically, I'm a medium and I'm still developing my abilities, so I often refer to my abilities as "medium rare."

This gift doesn't define who I am; it's just a part of me, as it is of so many others I've met since I wrote my first book, "*Ghosts and Spirits: Insights from a Medium*," published in December 2009.

For decades I didn't pay much attention to my abilities, because I didn't understand them and I wasn't spiritually or emotionally mature enough to do so. Years ago I fell in love and now I'm happily married. Since I met my partner, my abilities have increased a hundred-fold. I decided to learn much more about those who have passed, those who have crossed over into the light (spirits), and those who remain Earth-bound (ghosts). I've discovered a lot of information that has helped clarify my questions and have learned some interesting lessons about our life on Earth, and the ways in which those who have passed continue to communicate with those still living.

I've learned a lot more about ghosts and spirits since my first book was published. Both this and my previous book are different from other books on ghosts, in that they are very personal, and I always try and prove the things I've experienced. I wrote this book based on my abilities to communicate with those who have passed. Because I'm a scientist, I provided scientific explanations on the how and why ghosts and spirits exist and can communicate and will touch upon them here.

FOREWARD (Continued)

Being a medium means sometimes learning how to put together puzzle pieces of information from those who passed. Sometimes mediums get direct messages. Other times they get random words, pictures, names, dates and thoughts and they are usually very personal to the entity communicating with them. The trick is figuring out the message.

In this book, you'll read about a fantastic journey that a powerful spirit of a young man took me, my partner, and the spirit's father on during a one-day visit. The spirit's father was still grieving some 15 years after losing his son, but that changed after this visit. The son's spirit provided somewhat cryptic messages that his dad, my partner, and I were able to decipher. The experience was a great example of how mediumship works and how spirits communicate personal things we may really have to think about.

I've also learned lessons from spirits how to live better during our time on Earth. In this book, I show a more "human" side to ghosts and spirits, looking at them more as the living people who they were instead of supernatural entities.

I provide a recap of the basics for you here, including the how, what, where, and why of ghosts and spirits. You'll read about how anyone can receive or block signals, about spirits who stay around for their wakes, people who commit suicide, animal/pet communications, cemeteries, different types of haunting, how and why babies who have passed can communicate, and more experiences in various locations.

I always get a headache in the presence of a ghost or spirit (and there is a difference). You'll learn why towns near water have more activity. The book contains my personal experiences on and off ghost tours and in historic places as well as the experiences of some others; I explain what the ghost or spirit is trying to convey.

I was inspired to develop my abilities and help others after getting communications from my puppy Buzz, who was killed by a car when his leash opened. He's come back to me many times.

FOREWARD (Continued)

I hope that this book serves as a comfort to those who have lost loved ones and as proof that there's a life beyond. I also hope that it will provide you with a better understanding of the difference between Earth-bound ghosts and spirits who have passed into the light, and the methods they utilize to communicate with the living. It's important to maintain an open mind to things we don't understand. Our souls are living energy, and we are all connected while we are alive and even after we pass.

In this book, you'll read about adventures and message confirmations I have had with other mediums. I have so much respect and admiration for mediums and friends Barb Mallon, Ruth Larkin and Troy Cline.

You'll go on professional investigations with me and the Inspired Ghost Trackers of Maryland. The group is led by Margaret Ehrlich, and I am proud to be a member. I have a great deal of respect for the entire team.

I'm not a medium who makes appointments or charges people for readings, because I'm still learning how to refine my abilities and I tell people "the ghosts and spirits come to me when they come to me." There are a number of mediums who you can contact if you'd like personal readings, and you can find them using the Internet. I'm still working my way up to that stage of ability.

I would like to thank those who believe in my ability, especially my partner. A special thank you to our friend Jane, who so willingly volunteered to provide edits on this book.

If you have questions or stories you'd like to share please feel free to write me at Rgutro@gmail.com or write on my blog: *http://ghostsandspiritsinsights.blogspot.com/*

I look forward to hearing from you.

Rob Gutro

INTRODUCTION

I've learned a lot about this life and the next from my inherited ability to sense ghosts and spirits. I had my first encounter with a spirit as a teen. I have learned the difference between a ghost and a spirit, and this book will explain them. Through my experiences and those of others, I dig deeper into the what, who, when, where, and how entities communicate and share life lessons learned from talking with the dead.

Since I published my first book, I've had the opportunity to tour and meet people. I've learned that many people have the ability to receive messages. Open-mindedness is a key to that ability. I will discuss how being open to messages is important and show ways that Earth-bound ghosts and spirits attempt to communicate.

Ghosts differ from spirits in that they remain on Earth. Ghosts stay Earth-bound for many reasons, such as they experienced a sudden or violent death, they don't seem to understand they've passed on, they want revenge, they seek forgiveness for something they did, or have unfinished business.

I believe that God grants people and animals the ability to return to Earth; these are spirits. Once they pass into the light, spirits have the ability to return to those they loved for short periods of time to give them messages. I've sensed, seen, felt, and heard both Earth-bound ghosts and spirits who have crossed over. As I mentioned in my first book, I didn't ask for this ability but have come to realize it's inherited and it's a gift.

Everyone has the gift to communicate with those who passed. The key is to allow yourself to see the messages and not discount them with "logical explanations."

In this book I explain about messages I received from a friend's deceased stepfather that I passed onto her at the wake. Those messages were a comfort to her during her time of grief and loss. The ability to give someone comfort during the time of physical loss is a gift, and I encourage you to listen to the messages you get - so you can help others, too.

INTRODUCTION (CONT.)

My ability increased as I've grown older and my emotional state has been heightened. I'm no longer afraid of ghosts or spirits. I've found that fearing spirits prevents them from coming to you; however, they may come to someone else, as they can be persistent in getting their messages across.

I hope that this book provides insight and a better understanding of the spirit world. Hopefully it will allow you to open yourself up to receiving or seeing messages that you may have overlooked before. You just need to be aware of it.

CHAPTER 1: THE BASICS

What are the Differences Between Ghosts and Spirits?

Let me begin with stating that it's important to maintain an open mind to things we don't understand. Our souls are living energy, and we are all connected while we are alive and even after we pass.

Before I explain the differences between ghosts and spirits, is important to know that all of them were once living, breathing people like you. They may no longer be living in the physical sense, but they are living on another plane of existence and have the ability to communicate messages to those who are living.

Earth-bound ghosts and spirits differ in where they dwell and the methods they utilize to communicate with the living.

What are Spirits?

Spirits are the essence of people who lived on Earth like you and I, but whose physical body has died. Their energy has moved to the next plane of existence, what some think of as "heaven." Ghosts are composed of the same energy, but they have remained Earth-bound. I'll explain about ghosts shortly.

If you can dream of someone that means they've passed into the light. You can't dream of someone stuck on Earth. Spirits are at peace, while ghosts are not.

Usually, a person's energy will wait to cross to the next plane until after his/her wake or funeral, just to see who came to the service. After all, wouldn't you want to know who loved you enough to come to your service? It has also often been noted that when people are about to pass, the spirits of pre-deceased family members will appear to them to help them cross over. Sometimes, however, people can cross into the light right after they die.

There are many stories of people on their death beds who see dead relatives in the room with them, calling them into the light.

When my father passed in August 2008, I sensed that he stayed around all week during his services and saw him walk into the light at the cemetery. Within the light I saw a number of my relatives and three family dogs waiting for him on the other side. It was a visual memory I will never forget.

Who are spirits that communicate with us? Generally, these are spirits who we knew when they were alive and who passed away during our lifetime. A spirit could even be someone remotely connected to us, such as through a friend, co-worker, or neighbor. I've heard stories about a deceased child coming to his neighbor with a message for his living parent. Why? Most likely this is because the child's parent is still so grief-stricken that they are blocking out the messages the child's spirit is trying to send, so the child went to the neighbor with a message. Mediums can convey messages from spirits they don't know.

What abilities do spirits have that ghosts do not? Spirits who cross into the light have a power and ability that ghosts do not. Spirits can come back to loved ones whenever and wherever they want to bring messages. In fact, they can appear anywhere on Earth and even at multiple places at the same time. It goes beyond the boundaries of physics.

One of the interesting things I've learned is that at the minute a person passes, he or she might notify someone related to him or her, or even a friend, neighbor or acquaintance. I've read many stories of people who have seen a vision or heard a voice of someone they know at the exact same time the person died. Stories have been cataloged extensively in the book *"Hello From Heaven!"* written by Bill and Judy Guggenheim and published by Bantam Books in 1997.

Often, a person gets a vision of someone who just passed and a message that they've passed. The time of the visit is often within minutes of the death. Once we become a spirit, we are unbound from our physical bodies and can travel to those we're connected to instantaneously, and regardless of distance. Spirits also have the ability to visit multiple people at the same time, anywhere around the world.

What are Ghosts?

It's important to understand that Earth-bound ghosts were once living, breathing people who had hobbies and passions; perhaps had children, spouses, or pets and they worked for a living. They chose to remain behind rather than pass into the light, for some reason.

Ghosts feed off negative energy (fear, anxiety, pessimism) and can manifest themselves in the presence of these emotions. They typically have circumstances such as unfinished business, sudden death or a need for forgiveness from someone they've hurt in life.

Earth-bound ghosts are the ones who haunt places. They chose not to pass into the light and onto the next phase of life. Ghosts attach themselves to a place familiar to them or where they may have died tragically. Ghosts can also attach themselves to people and come home with them. They might also attach themselves to possessions such as a favorite chair, a dresser, a mattress (I had one experience with a ghost who apparently died on the mattress and stayed with it until I got her to go into the light), or a dresser. This is one reason why I don't like to go into antique stores; I can feel energies of the previous owners on the furniture.

Keep in mind that if a person loved an object immensely when he was alive, he might not want to let it go after he passes; and some of his energy might be left on that physical object.

Ghosts need not be directly or indirectly related to us to make their presence known. For example, ghosts can dwell in a house that once belonged to them, and another family has moved into. Perhaps, the ghost of the person who lived there didn't want to cross into the light and wanted to stay in their home.

Following is a true account of a ghost who was "stuck" on Earth searching for her baby who had died in childbirth with her. It serves as another example of what would cause a soul to remain Earthbound. Fortunately, I was able to cross her over into the light with the help of others.

3

Crossing Over an Earth-bound Ghost Seeking Her Baby

On the evening of August 12, 2011 my partner and I attended a talk at Inspired Ghost Trackers of Maryland. Also in attendance was our friend Troy Cline, also a medium. Unexpectedly, Troy and I wound up working together to free a troubled ghost.

That night the speakers talked about using a "ghost box," a radio of sorts that's wired to enable ghosts and spirits to talk through it. The hosts proved to the audience that the ghost box actually works.

Right after the intermission, Margaret Ehrlich, Inspired's founder, pulled me and Troy out of the audience and asked us to join her in the back. We stepped into the hallway, where Margaret told us of an entity in the ladies' room, of all places! Margaret said she was in there alone during the break and heard doors open and close. She said she felt a presence, but no living person was there.

Oddly, Inspired is located in a relatively new building and the group has been having meetings there for years. So, if there was a ghost in there, it had to come "with" someone that night.

Margaret and Ronda from Inspired Ghost Trackers made sure the restroom was empty, so I entered first. As I opened the door and stepped over the threshold, I got my tell-tale headache that told me there was an Earth-bound ghost or spirit in the women's bathroom. I get headaches because ghosts and spirits are made up of electrical energy. The headache is basically an electrical overload in my head from the entities' energy.

I stepped in and stopped at the sink as Troy walked toward the door. Still five feet away, he immediately stopped as an intense energy filled his chest, accompanied by a wave of emotion. Tears pooled in his eyes as he sensed longing and despair. After a few moments he looked past the door to see the look on my face; instantly confirming that we were feeling the same wave of energy. Both of us had chills and visible goose bumps. The entity (and it was a ghost) was standing right near us and drawing the warmth out of that part of the room. Next, Ronda and Margaret entered.

4

Ronda also experienced the cold sensation which seemed to intensify with every passing second. It was then that Kathy entered the bathroom and stood listening.

Almost at the same time, both Troy and I noted that the ghost was that of a woman. Then we asked why she was there. The woman immediately showed me a yellow house with white trim and had a wooden slat porch, painted white. This is where she came from.

Troy continued to sense sadness and tears. The woman was lost and didn't know what to do. She was an Earth-bound ghost who was trapped here. Troy remembered feeling an uncomfortable energy earlier that evening in the conference room where the ghost box talk was being given. The energy seemed to be attached to two women sitting near the back of the room. We soon figured out that the ghost came to the building with one of those women. The ghost, who told me her name was Nathalie, felt that the ghost tracking people understood her situation and could possibly help.

The cold energy in the bathroom continued to move to different locations. Troy next walked to the opposite side of the room where he sensed the ghost behind the last stall, sitting on the floor with her hands wrapped around her knees, not knowing what to do.

I have felt pain that some ghosts experienced when they died, but I had never felt anything like what happened next. Nathalie suddenly made my lower abdomen really hurt, to the point where I had to take in several deep breaths. That's when she told me that she died giving birth to a baby! Yes, in a weird way, I was experiencing the pain of childbirth. I asked her to stop sharing the pain and she did.

At that instant Troy began to sense an escalation in the ghost's emotional state that filled him with feelings of urgency, panic, and…guilt? He looked up and softly said, "She can't allow herself to go into light. She's afraid that if she does, she'll be leaving her baby behind." Nathalie was trapped on Earth because she stayed behind looking for her baby. What she didn't know was that her baby had died at birth, but had crossed over! I could sense her baby in the light telling me he was safe.

Neither the baby nor Nathalie's husband were able to communicate to Nathalie because spirits in the light cannot communicate with Earth-bound ghosts. They're on a different plane of existence. Because communications were impossible between planes, Nathalie thought the baby's energy was still Earth-bound like her.

Troy suddenly felt Nathalie holding his left arm and he became a conduit for her voice. Troy looked at me and started asking questions that were coursing through Nathalie's mind, "How can you help find my baby? What do we do next?"

I told him (as if I were speaking to Nathalie) she needs to cross over. Her baby had crossed into the light. Troy then said, "She still doesn't know what to do. She doesn't know how to cross over into the light." Ronda and I both said that we needed to focus on a portal of light opening up. We concentrated and I soon saw a white glow taking shape in the corner near the sink and mirrors. I asked Nathalie's husband to show himself and help her cross over.

Troy, Ronda, and I all saw the same thing. Troy said that Nathalie was still reluctant to go into the light. He said, "She wants to know if she can trust the people in the light. How can she know that they are telling her the truth - that her baby is there?" I replied to him (as Nathalie), "Because they are from the light. They will not lie to you." We encouraged her to step forward. Nathalie's husband and the infant she lost in childbirth were in the light. Standing next to them were Nathalie's parents. It was incredible and strange. It was like looking at people standing behind a giant, brilliant white donut, where the people on the other side were in the hole.

Troy and Ronda kept encouraging Nathalie to step closer, and I saw Nathalie stretch her right hand toward the light. That was the first time I visibly saw her. Minutes passed and we all sensed she moved into the light. Troy watched as a brilliant light appeared inside of Nathalie and grew until it completely transformed her into the light itself! Suddenly, although the air conditioning was blowing, an actual wave of warm air, about 10 degrees (Fahrenheit) warmer, hit all three of us. I looked surprised and turned to Troy who said "did you feel that?" I said, "The wave of warm air?", and he said "yes!" Ronda had also felt it.

The white light portal had closed, and Nathalie was finally at peace with her husband and the child she never met. We all stood there trying to understand what had just happened. We all breathed a sigh of relief and walked back into the room where the presentation was being held. After the presentation was over, Margaret asked Troy and me to share the story, which we did.

Margaret later said that she believed Kathy brought the ghost with her. Kathy told Margaret that she and her daughter were both sensitive to entities.

Margaret provided us with an explanation of where the ghost came from and how it got to the Ghost Tracker event. "When Kathy's daughter was in the Franklin Hospital after having her baby, she was lying in bed one night and heard someone calling her name. Kathy's daughter looked at the location where the voice seemed to be coming from (she didn't recognize the voice) and saw a mist."

We believe that Nathalie's ghost followed Kathy's daughter. When Kathy's daughter came home from the hospital and saw her mother, Nathalie's ghost followed Kathy to the Ghost Tracker's meeting knowing she would be in a good place where people understood what it meant to be trapped on Earth and perhaps would help her out." Fortunately, Nathalie's ghost was correct and we were able to cross her over.

What are Orbs?

Orbs are basically a simple form of light and may be the simplest form a ghost can assume or it could be energy connected to a ghost. Orbs appear as rounded droplets of light. In my experience, there were several instances when orbs have appeared in photos when I sensed a ghost nearby. I've conferred with experts at Inspired Ghost Trackers in Odenton, Maryland and they also still debate orbs. Some of the members said they have seen some orbs that are dark blue or even black.

Many ghost hunters don't put much stock in orbs. Frankly, it's easy to get excited about a rounded ball of light in a photo if you see one; however, reflections, dust, water droplets, and other aerosols (tiny objects floating in the air) can fool someone into thinking they photographed an orb.

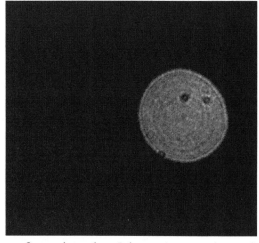

(PHOTO: Close up of orb outside the J.B. Jackson Building, Asheville, N.C. Credit: R. Gutro)

So, how do you tell the difference between those things and an orb? Orbs usually have colors and designs in them. In fact, some ghost hunters will attest that they've even seen faces in orbs. I haven't experienced seeing faces, but I've seen colors and designs that cannot possibly be dust. In one incredible photo that appears later in this book, you will clearly see the face of a murdered woman behind an orb.

According to Troy Taylor, author of *Ghosts on Film*, published by Whitechapel Productions Press (2005), many orbs are reflections of light on the camera lens, especially in areas that have bright light.

Taylor said that some low-end digital cameras have a "CMOS chip" that creates spots in low light photos. Those spots are mistaken for orbs. Reflections, dust, pollen, water droplets, etc., can all appear to resemble an orb. A good frame of reference is that if something appears all-white, it's very likely a reflection off one of those objects, or a reflection of the flash.

I took a trip to Asheville, North Carolina, and went on a ghost walk. During the walk I took many photos of various places with known haunted histories. In front of those places I felt a headache and realized there were entities present. The photos I took showed what appeared to be many orbs. The orbs had colors and designs within them. Those were orbs because of the colors and were not transparent. Some of the other rounded orbs in the photos appeared white, however, so I discounted those as dust or pollen.

The cover photo on this book shows an orb outside of the Thomas Wolfe house in Asheville. I took the photo using a digital camera on a night-time ghost walk in October 2010. The orb showed up in one of many photos taken of the outside of the house. The window of the room behind it was where Thomas Wolfe's brother's ghost is often seen. Wolfe's brother passed away at a young age and is reputed to still haunt the house. When I toured inside the house the following day, I did sense a ghost in the house.

If an orb appears in a photo at the time you sense a presence, that's confirmation that you've taken a picture of a true ghostly orb. That happened when I joined Inspired Ghost Trackers to investigate The Book Escape in Baltimore, Maryland. During our investigation in the basement I sensed a ghost named William in one particular corner. We took multiple photos. An orb (with colors) appeared in one of the photos (it was a dark, unlit corner) where I sensed William. That investigation is discussed in more detail later in this book (see: "The Book Escape, Baltimore, Maryland").

While touring the Riversdale Mansion in Riverdale, Maryland (no "s" in the name of the town, unlike the mansion name), I sensed the ghosts of a woman and a little girl in a large room. Margaret Ehrlich of Inspired Ghost Trackers had arranged that investigation and took photos when I mentioned the presence of these ghosts.

In the photo, four orbs actually appeared, confirming that there was a presence in the room; in fact, two more than I sensed. Apparently, I didn't sense the others because they were not as outspoken as the woman and the little girl. It turned out that four of the woman's children had died at a young age in the house, so the other orbs could have been those of her children. You can read more about Riversdale Mansion in the "Location" chapter.

During a private investigation, I sensed a lot of emotional energy and distress in the furnace room of a private residence. That was the location where two women may have put up a struggle before they were murdered. In a follow-up investigation conducted days later by Inspired Ghost Trackers of Maryland, an orb appeared with the face of a woman behind it. That story and photograph is featured in Chapter 11: What About Suicides/Murders.

Taking Photos of Orbs

Tour guides on ghost walks will tell you to take multiple photos of the same location inside or outside of a haunted place. Sometimes you'll get orbs with the colorful designs in them. Sometimes the orbs are not noticeable on the camera, but if you save the photo to your computer and enlarge it, the orbs become more apparent.

Why would orbs show in some photos and not others? Ghosts know that you're trying to find them. Why would they care? Because want your help to cross them into the light and free them from their earthly prison. That leads me to the next topic: why ghosts need your help.

Ghosts Need Help, Too

I enjoyed reading a book called *Helping Ghosts: A Guide to Understanding Lost Spirits* by Louis Charles. For anyone interested in earth-bound ghosts, this is a must-read. If you're a ghost hunter or have ever encountered ghosts, this book offers an excellent perspective that seems to get lost in most ghost hunting programs: ghosts were once human beings and they're trapped on Earth for some reason. They also need to cross over into the light because they don't belong here.

Being Earth-bound as a ghost is like being trapped in a prison as a living person. Think of a living person sentenced to solitary confinement in prison, with no contact to their loved ones on the outside. This is exactly what an Earth-bound ghost endures. The ghost is trapped on Earth and cannot communicate with his/her deceased relatives that crossed into the light. That's why digital recordings of ghosts will often have an entity saying "help me."

I actually "met" Louis through the Facebook page for my book on ghosts. Louis contacted me, and we've befriended each other through our authorship and our insight into ghosts. Louis really helps readers look at ghosts not so much as paranormal, but rather as people. He humanizes ghosts and explains that they all need our help to cross into the light, even the unfriendly ones.

Ghost hunting groups should have a medium or someone like Louis to help ghosts cross over. They don't belong here.

Louis Charles was born in Canton, Ohio and raised in a small farming community nearby. While growing up, he always had a fascination with ghosts and spirits. Through various careers, Louis Charles honed his skills in sales, marketing, speaking, and invention. He never lost his passion to learn more about ghosts and haunting. In 2004, he launched the Web site Angels & Ghosts (*www.angelsghosts.com/*) in order to better study ghosts and spirits. By using the submissions he received from around the world, Louis began comparing potential evidence shared in stories, images, videos, and audio recordings.

What Can / Should You Do to Help a Ghost?

In my opinion, if you see or sense an Earth-bound ghost, you have a responsibility to cross that ghost over into the light, where they can become a spirit and join their relatives. It is not that difficult to do, and it's the compassionate thing to do.

In June 2011, when I gave a talk at Inspired Ghost Trackers in Odenton, Maryland about three haunted local historic mansions, I told the audience that they need to try and cross ghosts over into the light.

One man said, "If I do that, I won't have any ghosts to hunt." I told him that was a selfish thing to say, because we're talking about the souls of people who are trapped on Earth and separated from their loved ones. There are many ghosts and they need our help!

I then asked Margaret Ehrlich and Ronda Dixon of Inspired Ghost Trackers, "What is the most common thing you hear in electronic voice phenomena when investigating ghosts?" They both answered that ghosts say, "Help me." Now why would ghosts be asking for help if they weren't trapped and didn't want to cross over to see their loved ones?

Think of how it feels to be a ghost: You die and make the decision to stay behind to try and help your loved ones deal with your death. Or you stay behind because you love your house and don't want to leave it, even in death. After a short time, you realize you missed your opportunity to move into the light (which appears either immediately or days after we die). You become trapped on Earth and don't know how to get to your loved ones who died before you. It seems that once an entity becomes an Earth-bound ghost for a short time, they forget how to cross over and need to be told. Louis Charles' book gave me a new awareness of my responsibility to help these people finally achieve peace.

So, how do you help ghosts cross over? If you sense an entity, tell them that you know they are trapped on Earth. Tell them that they should seek a funeral home, a hospital, or a cemetery where the light often appears for people who have recently passed away. They can enter the light there.

You can also picture a white light in the corner of a room. Focus and concentrate on it, while telling the ghost to enter into it to find peace. I crossed over a woman named Agnes in the waiting room of a hospital in Washington, D.C. this way. Of course, trying to talk with Agnes out loud while someone was sitting in the waiting room got me a couple of weird looks, but Agnes had been wandering around the hospital since she died of heart failure some time ago and just wanted to go home to her deceased relatives who had crossed over before her. As Margaret and Ronda said, a lot of ghosts say, "Help me." Now you can.

12

Are There Non-Human Ghosts and Spirits?

Ghosts and spirits are not limited to people. Throughout history there have been stories of ghostly horses trampling down dirt roads in the night, and wolves howling that aren't visible. Even dogs sometimes remain loyal to their late masters and ghost dogs have been seen sitting on top of gravesites.

My own puppy (who passed) was the inspiration for me to continue refining my abilities as he communicated with me many times as a spirit who crossed into the light. Animals such as dogs, cats and horses have been noted in ghost stories throughout history. Those animals all have the intelligence of a 5-year-old child. If children can come back, and they do, so can animals.

There are also dark entities that are said to never have had a human form. Fortunately, I have not encountered any of them. They are said to be demonic in nature. There are many books available that can provide you with insight into these beings. If you feel that the energies in your home are demonic, please call your local professional ghost hunting group to clear your home.

CHAPTER 2: ENERGY AND ENERGY BEINGS

Ghosts and spirits are both entities of energy. So where does the energy come from that becomes a ghost or a spirit? Two places: one is the soul where emotions dwell. The second place energy comes from is from our thoughts. In the physical body, thoughts generate electrical activity in the brain. Think about how doctors attach electrodes to a person's head to measure brain activity. Electroencephalography (EEG) is the recording of the brain's spontaneous electrical activity over a short period of time, usually about twenty to forty minutes. If you want more detail you can research it, but in short, brainwaves are electrical energy.

Energy

From a scientific perspective, energy cannot be destroyed only altered. The law of conservation of energy is a law of physics that says "the total amount of energy in an isolated system remains constant over time. The total energy is said to be conserved over time." The universe contains many different types of energy, including gamma rays, light-rays, x-rays, ultraviolet, infrared and visible light and more.

In the law of conservation of energy, "for an isolated system, the law means that energy can change its location within the system" (think of that in terms of the soul's energy moving from the physical body to join the energy of the universe or stay Earth-bound). The law also states "energy can also change form within the system, for instance chemical energy can become kinetic energy, but that energy can be neither created nor destroyed."

So, if energy can't be destroyed what happens to the energy of those brainwaves when our body dies? I believe that it, in combination with the energy of our soul's transition into an earthbound ghost or a spirit that crosses into the light.

When our physical bodies die, the energy in our soul and mind make a decision in death whether to stay on Earth as an Earth-bound ghost, or to move into the light and become a spirit.

Once we die we gain an awareness of what was right and wrong in the way in which we lived on Earth. Sometimes, when people die, they become instantly aware they wronged someone when alive, so they stay Earth-bound to try and obtain forgiveness.

So, how do we gain all that knowledge of right and wrong? How do we become aware of all of the things happening around the world at the same time, or things affecting our friends and family? The answer lies in energy. Just as the universe is composed of matter and energy (and light energy or dark matter), our individual energies merge with that of the cosmos. We instantly gain knowledge of everything in the cosmos when we die because our energy becomes part of that. It's like being plugged in to a socket of knowledge. Energy is all interconnected and that's what happens to our awareness. We instantly know what is good and what is evil.

Energies That Affect Ghosts and Spirits

Now that we know that ghosts and spirits are beings of energy, we can understand that giving them more energy enables them to communicate with us. Think of a ghost as a marionette with no one pulling its strings. Until there is someone "pulling the strings" to make the marionette move the ghost sits idle. By bringing physical or emotional energy, we provide the catalyst that "pulls the strings" of a ghost and give it power to move.

There are a variety of energies that affect ghosts and spirits and enable them to communicate. Physical energies such as water, electricity, heat, and light help "power up" Earth-bound ghosts and spirits. My own father, during the week of his passing, manipulated the electricity in my mother's house to let her know that he was still around. I wrote about those experiences in my first book. Those energies provide ghosts or spirits with the ability to interact and give signals to the living. They can also manipulate those energies.

Emotional energy is the other source of power for ghosts and spirits. Positive emotions are used by spirits who have crossed into the light, while negative energies assist Earth-bound ghosts. Positive energies are good emotions such as love and hope. Negative energies are fear, anxiety, hatred, and pessimism.

Spirits cannot use negative energy to appear and manifest; only Earth-bound ghosts use negative energy. Later in the book, you'll read about how a woman's love for her late son gave him the energy to appear near his grave site when she visited it. On the flip side, if you enter an old house and feel anxiety and fear it might be haunted, your anxiety can help a ghost (negative energy) manifest. That's because your negative emotions add power to the entity.

Negative energy between people, such as a married couple who bickers or fights, provides a good environment for Earth-bound ghost to energize. I read such a story from Jason Hawes and Grant Wilson in Ghost Hunting by Pocket Books, 2007.

Types of Hauntings

There are two types of hauntings: "intelligent" and "residual." In intelligent hauntings, ghosts have independent thought and can do things, such as move objects, make noises, make appearances and directly respond to questions asked by a living person.

Professional ghost hunters often use equipment to detect electronic voice phenomena (EVP). An EVP is an audible response to a direct question. If you get a reply to a question, then you are dealing with an intelligent haunting and the entity knows what it is doing.

In 2011, I investigated a bookstore in Baltimore, Maryland, and sensed a male ghost. The digital recorder held by one of the Inspired Ghost Trackers also present recorded a strong male voice saying, "get out." That's an intelligent haunting. He knew that we were in his space, he was aware that we were looking for him and he didn't want us there.

Residual hauntings are simply images of the past that contain so much emotional energy in a location at one time that they happen over and over again, like a tape playing. One example is a woman in the 1800s continually going to the second floor window of a coastal home, looking out over the ocean in anticipation of her naval captain husband's return from sea. If that captain died at sea, the widow would continue to go back to that window, even in death. A residual haunting can also mean that a ghost's energy is attached to an object the person loved during his lifetime.

Residual hauntings pose no threat and do not have the ability to interact with the living, answer questions, turn lights off and on, throw things, etc. I encountered that kind of energy when visiting an historic home in Quincy, Massachusetts and I kept seeing a horse-drawn carriage pull up in front of the house over and over. Residual hauntings are simply energies of events from a time passed that had so much emotion, that it happens over and over, like an imprint of a glass left on a table.

Now that we know about the different types of hauntings, it is important to know what happens when we help Earth-bound ghosts cross into the light.

What is Crossing into the Light?

What is "crossing into the light?" I believe that crossing into the light means our energies join the energies of the universe. When that happens, we instantly develop an awareness of everything within the universe. We understand good and evil and we gain the knowledge of the cosmos.

A spirit who has crossed into the light can see what's happening anywhere around the world and in multiple places at one time. It goes beyond our physical limitations. Think of the magnetic field that surrounds the Earth. If part of your energy merges with that field, your conscience would be able to "see" what is happening anywhere around the globe.

By crossing into the light after death, not only does your energy connect directly to that of the cosmos, but it enables the spirit to communicate with anyone on Earth at any location. This is quite different from an Earth-bound ghost, because ghosts are usually restricted to the location in which they chose to dwell or haunt. Being a spirit in the light also brings us an ability to watch over those on Earth, whereas ghosts do not have that power.

In fact, when an energy stays behind as a ghost to help their family deal with the grief of their passing, the ghost creates negative energy in the household.

17

The negative energy given off by the ghost can create bad feelings, nervousness, sleeplessness, aggravation, tension and arguments. Interestingly, all of these emotions and feelings will in turn, energize the ghost. It's a vicious cycle, and I'll explain more about the types of energies next.

The most important thing to draw from this is that you must encourage your late friends and family members to cross into the light. It is there they will find peace and be with loved ones who have crossed over. Being an earth-bound ghost is like being trapped in a solitary confinement of a prison, with no way to communicate with any loved ones. Ghosts can only communicate with those who come to them. Spirits, however, can communicate to anyone anywhere.

What is "In the Light"?

Our consciousness and soul translate into energy when we pass and once we move into the light, we become one with the energy that runs through the cosmos. When we cross over we develop an immediate awareness of what was right and wrong about how we lived on Earth.

So what is "in the light"? I understand that spirits do have "jobs" on the other side. They often show mediums where they dwell, usually in fields with blue sky above. Is that actually where they live? No. But it's a place of peace that we on Earth can understand and identify with.

It is my understanding that there are at least three levels on the other side. Which level you attain depends on how well you learned your lessons on Earth.

The first level is the lowest level. It is where people who did not live a good life dwell and they atone for their bad behavior. These are people who were evil or did bad things during their time on Earth. However, they now have full awareness that the way in which they lived on Earth was not good for them or others.

Spirits that dwell on the first level are those who lived with hatred in their hearts, people who commit crimes against others, people who hold grudges, oppress others, do not treat others equally, discriminate, and hate, all linger here hoping for forgiveness... before they go back to Earth to try again. Yes, spirits on the lowest level come back to Earth in human form and go through life again, hoping to learn lessons and get to the second level in the light. I often joke that people who cut me off in traffic "are going to be coming back again and again."

The second level is where many spirits dwell. It is a place where people who lived decent lives on Earth dwell in the spirit world. These are spirits of people who learned lessons in life and treated others well. Souls in this level have the chance to go back to Earth to learn more lessons, but because this is a comfortable place (similar to what people call "heaven"), they sometimes don't want to leave and return to Earth. Usually, however, they do return to Earth to learn more lessons. Life on Earth is a continual learning process and everything we face is something we need to face to make us spiritually stronger and achieve a higher level in the afterlife.

The third level is one of perfection. There are few souls in this realm. Souls like Jesus and Mohammad. This is a level where the souls do not return to Earth, as there are no other lessons to learn.

There are a number of mediums and others who have received information about the levels of the afterlife. It is difficult to pinpoint exactly how many levels there are in the light, but we do know there are multiple levels, and they are based on Earthly behaviors and lessons learned.

The Afterlife Forum.com explains levels in the afterlife in this manner: "Basically, all the levels are in the same place, just at a different level of spiritual vibration. The higher a person's level of spiritual vibration, the higher the level to which he/she belongs. The way that you elevate your spiritual vibration level is by coming to earth to learn lessons in love and forgiveness." That Web site cites 7 levels in the afterlife. Everyone has a different opinion - and there's no clear answer to the number of levels.

Other cultures have similar beliefs. Buddhists believe there are six levels of existence. Some people in Japan believe there are three levels of the afterlife: lower, middle, and higher. Those levels are like the Christian ideas of hell, heaven and perfection. The Japanese belief is that people who are negative or morally corrupt (or evil) go to the lowest area. They can't get to the higher areas, closer to perfection, until they come back to Earth (reincarnated) and live another life, going through life's trials and maybe getting it more "right." This is the same theology that used to be in the early Christian Bible, before it was edited out. It is clear, however, that people go to different levels based on the way they lived on Earth.

In the light, spirits are judged for their behavior on Earth and their conscience places them on different "levels" in the light. As Betty Eadie mentioned in Embraced by the Light (1992, Gold Leaf Press), we choose to come back to Earth to try and live a better life the next go 'round.

Before we come back in another life we know the challenges we're going to face; i.e., with a physical or mental disorder, healthy yet impoverished, struggling to find love, a decade-long search for a good job, even being born into a difficult family all because we know there's a lesson we need to learn to achieve a higher level of understanding.

Spirits do return to Earth in another life to do a better job of learning how to live. We must continue to show more love and compassion for each other, and be more loving, thankful, and optimistic about life, no matter what you're dealt.

The bottom line is that we must all respect each other. We are all equal. We all deserve the same rights. The same freedoms. The same joys. To deny someone of something by using your authority, pushing your religious views on other, or using your wealth to control others is wrong. If you don't believe me, you will learn it when your earthly life is over.

CHAPTER 3: RECEIVING SIGNALS

Everyone has the ability to receive messages and communicate with ghosts and spirits. I mentioned in my previous book how sensitivity to ghosts and spirits can run in families, but that doesn't mean it's limited to those families.

I've learned a lot about sensing ghosts and spirits since I wrote my last book. Much of this enlightenment occurred while touring with my book and meeting people. Many people shared their experiences with ghosts, premonitions, or what they thought were coincidences (there are no such thing as you'll understand through reading this book). I've also learned that there are many people that have some level of abilities as a medium. They've sensed ghosts or spirits or received and understood various signs, and want to know how to refine their abilities.

In my case, the gift to sense and communicate with those who have passed is inherited. My mother and grandfather have it. Other family members, however, do not seem to have the ability either because they choose not to believe or acknowledge it or they unintentionally block messages (which is very likely the case). These other family members are logical thinkers and are not as emotional as I am, two factors that contribute to blocking messages from those who have passed.

There are a number of factors involved in reading or picking up the signals that ghosts and spirits use to convey to us. First, blocking factors need to be eliminated. Guilt, grief and fear block spirit communications. Second, if you're in a logical thinking mindset, you cannot receive messages. That's why most spirits come to us in our dreams, when our logical mind is asleep. Third, if we can't concentrate or achieve peace of mind, then we block messages. That happens to me often. In fact, the only times I can achieve that peace is in the shower, driving, or getting ready for bed.

There are several ways people can sense or communicate with spirits. They can be clairsentient, clairvoyant or clairaudient. People or mediums who can read spirits can be more than one of the above.

Although my abilities are limited and not yet fully developed, I've experienced clairsentience, clairvoyance, and clairaudience.

Clairsentience means that you can sense when a spirit is in the room. *Clairvoyance* is the ability to see spirits, people, colors, objects, and even scenes that a spirit wants a person to see in order to communicate thoughts or ideas to the medium. It's not actually seeing these things in a room, for example, but rather, seeing them in your mind. Messages come to me sometimes as images or words. Many of them may not make sense to me (or another medium), so the messages have to be interpreted by the person they are intended for. *Clairaudience* is the ability to hear clearly. A clairaudient hears sounds such as music, speaking, and laughter.

One of the best books I've read about everyone having the ability to sense spirits (those who have crossed into the light) deals with research done on after death communications (ADCs). The book *Hello From Heaven!* by Bill and Judy Guggenheim, has over 3,000 short stories of average people who have sensed, heard, smelled, been touched by, dreamt of, received a telephone call from, seen symbols or experienced strange electronic occurrences from someone close to them who had passed away.

That book provides great insight into many of the ways in which spirits communicate, and I recommend it to anyone who has lost a loved one. Two weeks after I bought it, I learned that I was guided to buy it from the spirit of my partner's late partner, Ed. You'll read about the amazing journey that Ed took me and others on in a later chapter.

Hello From Heaven! gives examples of different ways that spirits communicate with the living to give messages that they are okay on the other side. Message deliveries range from dreams to twilight (when you're half-awake and half-asleep) to wide-awake visible experiences. Experiences usually occur when we are relaxed.

Messages from the other side can come as touches, cold or hot embraces from spirits, audible words or noises, or scents associated with someone who passed (like a perfume, tobacco or flowers).

Messages can also be visible signs or symbols that mean something personal to the person who passed, such as a special jar of coins that had a strange name on the label. I'll explain that story in the chapter about Ed (my partner's late partner) and how it took awhile to figure it out. That's how I get a lot of my messages - through pictures and symbols - and they're almost always personal. It's up to the person who the messages are for to help figure out what they mean, and that's the challenge of mediumship.

It is important to note that Earth-bound ghosts do not have many of these capabilities. Only entities that have crossed into the light can perform all of these things and anywhere on Earth. Ghosts can provide audible signs (speaking, creaking floors), move physical objects, and make appearances.

Ghosts, however, are usually limited to performing signs in the place in which they dwell or haunt (unless they've followed you). Ghosts usually dwell in those places where they were comfortable or enjoyed being in during their time on Earth.

How Guilt, Grief, Logic Block Spirit Messages

In April 2010 when I was still promoting my first book, I learned that Troy, a colleague and friend also happens to be a developing medium. The revelation came about through an email, which I now understand was the work of a spirit.

Troy and I had worked for the same employer and casually known each other for 5 years never having gone to lunch. So how did Troy and I learn about each other's medium abilities?

In March 2010 I saw a notification from the Internet network "Linked In." Most of the time I don't read them, but this time I clicked the message open and read it. Troy's name was there, and it said he had been promoted. Even though it had been 3 or so years since I'd last seen him, I emailed and congratulated him and asked to meet for lunch. Why? I'm certain it was a spirit of someone who loves him that wanted us to meet, so I could help awaken his awareness of his abilities.

That same spirit person or pet also prompted me to open up to him about my abilities so that he could reveal the same. There are NO such things as coincidences.

Troy and I met for lunch and talked about work-related things. Then I mentioned that I had written a book about ghosts and spirits. Troy was surprised at my abilities because he also had the same abilities! He explained to me how he had many different experiences but had not concentrated on his abilities.

Troy and I talked about dogs and how my puppy Buzz (who was killed in 2005 when his leash opened and he ran in front of an oncoming car) has come to me many times. Troy lamented that his childhood dog, Pete, hadn't come to him at all, despite their strong bond. Troy went on to tell me that he felt guilty for leaving the dog with his parents when he went off to college. He said the last three years of the dog's life were spent with his parents and they didn't have a fenced-in yard, so they often put "Pete" on a long chain in their backyard. Troy said that Pete would be very excited to see him when Troy came home on break from college, and he felt badly that he couldn't share the days together anymore with his canine companion now that he was in college.

I explained to Troy that a dog's love is unconditional. Dogs are forever devoted to their owners, and when they cross over that love is still there and always will be. Troy thought about it for a couple of minutes and acknowledged that the love that he had for his dog Pete is still as strong as it was when he was alive. I watched Troy's face light up.

When I returned to my office, I received the following email from Troy, because his guilt had left him and Pete was finally able to come through:

> *April 7 at 3:07 pm   Right after lunch today, my dog Pete showed up again. This time I realized that the guilt that I had been carrying about not being with him during the last few years of his life had actually blocked my bond with him. I didn't realize the blockage existed...until today. I immediately reconnected with 'Pete.'*

When I did, I could feel him yelping with excitement that we were back together! I was overwhelmed. Thanks for sharing your energy today. It really made an 'unexpected' difference. :)

My email back was: April 7 at 3:37 pm Troy - That is awesome about Pete! Once you realized that your guilt wasn't founded, it opened you up. That's exactly what we were talking about how guilt, emotion or grieving can block a spirit's attempts to communicate. There are a lot of reasons why you and I have connected. I believe that we're helping each other enhance our abilities. (I later learned how true that would be when Troy and I were able to validate each other's experiences).

The lesson from this story about Troy is that if you have grief and guilt over the passing of a loved one, you have to realize that they are truly in a better place. They do not want the living to feel guilt, grief or remorse. Those things are detrimental to people trying to live their lives and they block the signs and messages from the spirits trying to communicate with the living.

It is easy to say to someone "don't feel guilty" about not being there when someone died. People who pass know that the living cannot be around at all times, and it's not as important to be in a room at the exact moment someone passes as it is to treat them well when they are alive. The next chapter contains a moving story that I experienced in the spring of 2011, when my partner and I went to Virginia. We took the trip to meet the father of my partner's late partner, Ed (who died in 1996). Ed's dad still felt guilt even after 15 years, and Ed's visit and signs through me would be enough to break through that guilt.

The Importance State of Mind in Receiving Messages

An Aunt's First Visit Since 1996

The keys to receiving messages are meditation, a peaceful mind, and concentration. That means being free of stress for a time. In today's world it's hard to find time to do these!

For me, the only times I can achieve peace or have time to concentrate is when I'm in the shower, sitting in front of the computer answering emails, or driving to work. Those are the times I usually receive messages. If you want to receive messages, you need to find "quiet time," and that can be in the places I mentioned, or anywhere you can relax.

For example, one morning in 2010, I was relaxed while driving to work and received a message. I was listening to an old CD of Barbara Mandrell's greatest hits (I love classic country music). The song "If loving you is wrong (I don't want to be right)" came on.

That song reminded me of my Aunt Tillie, because before she passed, she was seeing a man who was separated from his wife and she always thought it was "wrong" (it was decades ago) but couldn't resist his charms. That man passed before my aunt did.

Music is one of the ways that spirits will communicate with us, through a song play that reminds us of them. If a song comes on the radio that reminds you of someone who passed away, it's because they wanted you to hear it.

As the song started, I suddenly received a message from my aunt. She told me "thank you" for getting my mother (her sister) to forgive her for some not-so-nice things she did to my mom. Back in 1996, when I lived in Kentucky, my aunt came to me as a dark figure (trapped on Earth in a self-imposed exile and apparently feeling shame and guilt for those things she did when alive) and begged me to help get her sister's forgiveness. It wasn't until years later that I was able to convince my mom to give that forgiveness, and my aunt was able to cross over into the light. My aunt let me know she's now happily with her husband, my late uncle Richard.

She next showed me the old 1967 car with black leather interior that she and Uncle Richard would drive my younger brother and me around in when we stayed with them on weekends. They used to sing the old Bobby Vinton song, "Red Roses for a Blue Lady" (that they loved). They then reminded me of another song they loved by Marty Robbins called, "A White Sport Coat and a Pink Carnation," that they also used to sing in the car.

I asked my aunt if she was at peace, and suddenly the CD playing that Barbara Mandrell song skipped four times fast (her way of saying "yes.") The CD played fine for another 30 seconds, then I asked if she was happy on the other side and the CD skipped again! Another "Yes" answer. I then saw a blue blouse that she showed me that she had apparently taken of my mom's when she was alive and had regrets about it. The CD was then playing another song without skipping. I then asked my aunt's spirit one more question and as an answer, the CD suddenly skipped 4 times fast indicating a "yes!" The rest of the CD didn't skip at all, so it's obvious she was manipulating the CD player to answer me.

When I received her answers, I was "forced" to smile. It was odd and I my aunt assuring me she's fine and happy on the other side.

I tell this story because it brings up several points: One, spirits can use music to remind us of them. Two, spirits can give us images to show that they are happy, content, or unhappy. Three, spirits can manipulate electronics to provide messages. Whether it is skipping a CD, making lights go on and off, or some other sign from electronic manipulation, they are all things that spirits can do to give messages. The key to all of this is being open-minded enough to understand that these things are NOT coincidences. There are no such things as coincidences.

Distractions Inhibit Receiving Messages

If you're a sensitive person and have the ability to receive messages from ghosts and spirits, it's very easy for distractions to interfere with your abilities. Over the months of December 2010 and January 2011, I dealt with situations that seemed to block out my abilities, not because I didn't pay attention, but because I was pre-occupied with what was happening in the real world. Think of standing in the middle of a concert and trying to hear someone talking with you from 10 rows behind you - it's impossible. That's what everyday distractions do to our ability to hear messages from ghosts or spirits.

During those two hectic months, my dad provided me a sign through my mother's actions. Before my mother visited for the holidays, my dad's spirit led my mother to a brand new wallet he had purchased for himself the year he passed (in 2008). She found it and said she immediately thought I would want it, which was likely a suggestion from my dad. So, she gave it to me for Christmas, and that's a present I will never forget.

My mother visited over the holidays in 2011 and stayed with us. She was suffering from short term memory loss and asked the same question several times in 30 minutes. Her long-term memory was fine, but she had become impatient and short-fused. I understand it is part of the illness, but it was challenging to deal with over the holidays. Because of the extra care and constant attention, I was unable to receive messages from spirits or ghosts.

We work with two rescues and see dogs come to them in horrible condition. In December 2010, Coast-to-Coast Dachshund rescue asked us to take in a foster dog named "Sprite." This poor little senior Dachshund belonged to an elderly couple, one of whom passed away. Sprite was 13 years old and was in rough shape: underweight with worms and fleas. He and had not seen a vet in 5 years.

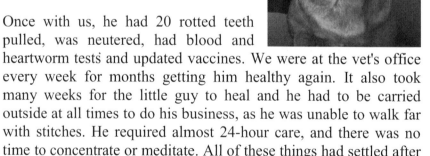

(PHOTO: Our foster dog Sprite that we adopted in 2011. Credit: R.Gutro)

Once with us, he had 20 rotted teeth pulled, was neutered, had blood and heartworm tests and updated vaccines. We were at the vet's office every week for months getting him healthy again. It also took many weeks for the little guy to heal and he had to be carried outside at all times to do his business, as he was unable to walk far with stitches. He required almost 24-hour care, and there was no time to concentrate or meditate. All of these things had settled after my mother returned home and Sprite was re-house trained.

Life is filled with distractions. In order to receive messages, it is important to try and find quiet time and important for your sanity!

Negative Energy Affects Sensitive People

Whenever I do a book tour, people come up to me and share their experiences. In 2010, one woman talked to me about her abilities as a developing medium. We talked about how ghosts utilize negative emotional energy and spirits (those who have crossed over into the light) use positive emotional energy to power up. She told me that she's an emotional person. She brought up an interesting point about how being around people who are pessimistic tends to make her physically sick. This is can be true for all people.

The person she mentioned who was draining her was her elderly mother, who had grown from a loving mother into someone who was bitter, negative, and never had a good word to say. If you work with negative people or have them in your family, try and limit contact with them as much as possible (I know this can be difficult). Negative-minded people want to be around positive people because they hope it will "rub off" on them. That doesn't happen, however. Negative people continue to be negative and wear down the positive people. People who choose to be down and negative generally need therapy.

We all have control over how we view life, and I have known people in horrible situations who remained optimistic and it made life better.

One of my dear friends battled stage four cancer and remained happy, hopeful, and optimistic until the day she passed. Sarah was a joy to be around. I can't imagine being in a worse position that she was, having learned about her cancer just 6 months before she passed, yet she was a beacon of love throughout that short time she had left on Earth. I dedicated this book to her.

The woman I met that day on the book tour in 2010 mentioned that when she visited her intensely pessimistic mother, she couldn't stay long periods of time, because the negativity physically affected her. I experienced the same thing in 2009, when I visited and stayed with a negative, bitter person for two days. I came home physically sick to my stomach and with a lingering headache.

Sensitive people and mediums feel negativity and positivity more than the average person.

Be good to yourself and try not to put yourself in a situation where you cannot get away from a negative person. Your mental and physical well-being depends on it, not to mention your ability to receive messages from those who have passed.

Logical Thinking Seeks Explanations

I received an email from a gentleman asking about how to determine whether his parents are at peace. His background is similar to mine, a background in science, so we were both "taught" to be logical thinkers. Because our logical mind tries to explain things, usually discards unexplainable events, and calls things "coincidences," we don't recognize signs from spirits (those who have passed into the light).

For the person who doesn't have a medium's abilities, the only way that spirits of passed loved ones can communicate in dreams. In fact, in this man's case, both parents did appear in his dreams.

Usually within the first year or two after a loved one has passed, they tend to appear in a relative's dreams. However, the appearances tend to fade over time. I believe that spirits hope that after that amount of time, the living relative moves on with their lives and stops grieving. It's important that we who are left behind understand these signs and that our loved ones who pass want us to move on. We can call to those who have passed, and they will hear us.

CHAPTER 4: AMAZING EXPERIENCE OF HOW MEDIUMSHIP WORKS

Mediumship is detective work, but the clues are usually difficult to decipher, so often they're dismissed. For example, if a spirit stops a clock at the exact same time they died, which has happened often, a loved one could be quick to say, "The battery must've died." The following adventure is an example of how paying attention to signs provides great comfort to those left behind.

Son Provides Proof and Comforts His Father

This chapter contains one of the most amazing and rewarding events I've experienced as a medium. Because I'm still honing my abilities, I'm still amazed when I can prove messages I receive. The following events which happened in the spring of 2011, show that signs, words, and symbols that a medium gets from a departed loved one may not make immediate sense. In fact, none may make sense! In this case, my partner's late partner (Ed) came to me several times with words, pictures, and messages that didn't make sense until I connected with several people who were close to him when he was alive.

In March 2011, I was finally able to meet Ed's family in central Virginia. Ed passed in 1996 and there was some question about whether or not he had intentionally taken his own life, but that was cleared up on this trip, through Ed's many messages.

The day before we left for the three-day weekend to visit Ed's family, I was in the bathroom shaving (with the water running, which is energy that helps spirits manifest) and Ed's spirit came to me. I was getting ready for work, so I was only thinking of getting organized and getting out the door when I heard Ed tell me a couple of things. He repeated things several times: "jingle" and "get the book." He showed me a blue-jacketed, bound book. At the time I was uncertain what those messages meant. That night I asked my partner if the messages made sense - they didn't. Although he and his partner had been together for about 12 years, he didn't know the significance of those two things. That mystery would have to wait.

We departed for our weekend on Friday, March 18, and arrived by early evening at a wonderful bed and breakfast called "Chestnut Hill" in Orange, Virginia. We dined in the Silk Mill Restaurant and over dinner, started talking about Ed. After a couple of minutes, I started getting the tell-tale headache in the back left side of my head. The headache occurs as a result of an overload of electrical energy in my brain, as a result of a ghost or spirit nearby.

Ed had joined us for dinner, in a manner of speaking, and he really wanted in on the conversation. After all, we were talking about him so why wouldn't he want to listen? Spirits can be funny that way, so be careful about what you say about those who have passed. They can hear you.

During dinner, Ed conveyed his excitement and happiness that I was finally going to meet his father, because I could share messages that would hopefully help his dad move on from the intense grief he had been feeling since Ed had passed some 15 years before. There was so much emotion from Ed that I teared up twice over dinner. There was an amazing amount of energy and love coming from Ed.

Ed provided some additional information besides the "jingle" and "book" that he gave me the day before. He showed me an old soda fountain located in an old pharmacy. I had no idea what that meant until I told my partner, who mentioned that Ed's dad was a pharmacist. However, we didn't know what the soda fountain meant... until later.

Ed also showed me what looked like a rowboat on the side of a river or lake. But I also kept getting the word "kayak." I was unsure how a rowboat could be considered a kayak, but I told my partner Tom what the messages were. He couldn't understand either, but we would later know how that was possible. Ed told me that his dad needed to "turn on his computer and look through it to help confirm that his passing was an accident." I learned that Ed's father still had Ed's computer (since 1996) but couldn't get into it because he didn't have the password. Ed also mentioned "duke or duchess," which we would not be able to confirm.

32

The next day, we finally met Ed's dad at the cemetery where Ed was buried. Tom had been there several times and knew where it was. When we got out of our car, I immediately developed the tell-tale headache that a spirit (or ghost) was present. Ed was back again. The love I felt from Ed's spirit overwhelmed me. Immediately afterward, I was startled when I felt a cold hand on my left shoulder! There was no one behind me, and I knew it was Ed. I stood still for a minute. Tom had walked to the grave and asked what I was doing standing there. I explained what happened.

Ed's dad pulled up minutes later and joined us at Ed's grave. Previously, he had only known me through phone calls and by reading about Ed's earlier messages that I wrote about in my first book. Ed's dad and Tom looked down at the grave site and Ed's spirit made me say out loud, "I'm not down there, I'm standing right next to you!" They just looked at me. Ed's dad then looked over the vast cemetery that allowed only plaques and not gravestones, and said "Ed always said to make sure he wasn't ever buried in a cow pasture. This looks like a cow pasture." It was a welcome break to the emotion of the moment.

We left the cemetery and followed Ed's dad back to his house, where we talked about the other signs Ed had given me. Tom told us that every day for the entire week before our trip, he had asked Ed to give me signs and he certainly had. The lesson here for everyone is that if you want signs from your loved ones who passed, ask them. Spirits can hear you, and they will respond.

Ed's dad couldn't identify the boat, jingle, "duke" or "duchess," or the blue book, but he does have many of Ed's books. He said he would check through them for something like a "blue-bound book." He acknowledged he had the computer but no password. I urged him to bring it to a computer service.

As we were sitting there talking, Ed gave me a couple of other messages. Ed's spirit kept telling me that he is now with "granny," so I asked Ed's dad if he used to call his grandmother (his father's mother) "Granny." Ed's dad said, "Ed called my mother 'Granny.'" Ed's "Granny" had passed away late last year, and he was telling us that he's with her on the other side.

The big comfort came when Ed told me to tell his dad, "It was an accident." Ed's death was the result of an interaction of prescription medications, and it was uncertain if it was an accident or if he took his own life. Ed also made me say, "I didn't mean it." His dad took great comfort in hearing that because he had been grieving for 15 years. "I knew it," his dad said.

Ed's father immediately identified the old soda fountain and old pharmacy. He worked as a pharmacist before he retired. As a young man, he worked as a "soda jerk" at a pharmacy lunch counter. He told me that just earlier that week, he was talking with some of his old friends who also worked as soda jerks. Ed was trying to tell me that he was there listening to that conversation his dad was having with his old friends who shared that profession!

Another of Ed's signs told me that he was with his brother earlier that week. When we drove to Ed's brother's house, sitting in the driveway was a brand new boat! The boat was unlike one I've ever seen. When we greeted Ed's brother, he told us that the boat was "like a rowboat" because you use oars. He said that it can be used in whitewater rafting and he just had it shipped from Colorado. He talked about how he loves going on his new boat to fish. This was the "rowboat" that Ed showed me but I didn't understand the "kayak" part. I also didn't say anything about it because I was unsure if Ed's brother believed in spirits giving messages to the living, so we went in the house briefly and met their children.

We went in the house for a short time and stopped on the front stairs as we were leaving. For some reason, Ed's brother mentioned his boat again and said, "It's made of plastic and it's like a kayak." Tom and I looked at each other wide-eyed and didn't say anything. That was the "rowboat/kayak" that Ed had indeed shown me!

Ed's brother caught the look of surprise and said "Have you guys been kayaking?" I thought quickly and told him we did go on a kayak ride in Puerto Rico through a bioluminescent bay (which I recommend). The conversation changed again and we said goodbye. Driving off, Ed's father, Tom and I immediately knew that Ed's spirit was trying to tell us that he knew his brother bought this new boat and was excited about it. We were all amazed.

As we were driving to see Ed's old pickup truck (which was still operational and parked at his brother's business), Ed's dad said, "I know what "jingle" means!" He told us that Ed had two containers where he put coins. One was a clear glass jar and the other was what looked like a coffee container. The coffee container clearly said, "Jingle Java." This is the "jingle" that had a special meaning for Ed because he used it every day, filling it with coins! It now sits in his dad's house with the other jar of change, both of which remain untouched since Ed passed in 1996.

We would later return to Ed's dad's house and I took a picture of the "Jingle Java" coin can. It turns out that it was a specially made gift from a graphics design company, specifically for Ed. There's even a dedication imprinted on the side of it.

(PHOTO: Ed's "Jingle Java" coin can. Credit: R.Gutro)

I was again in awe of the messages Ed was conveying and how these random images and words were making total sense with his family.

We visited Ed's old truck and when I touched it, I was able to sense his energy on it. People who pass leave residual energy on items they liked in life. Ed's dad said that Ed had loved this truck. I've sensed residual energy on pieces of furniture, and in homes that have "residual haunting" where events replay over and over and the entity cannot interact with the living. I wound up taking a photo of Tom and Ed's dad in front of the truck because it meant so much to Ed.

We spent a couple more hours together and Ed's dad took us on a tour of the town. After dinner we returned to Ed's dad's house. Tom and Ed's dad leafed through a couple of Ed's books and Tom found a half-completed poem in one of them (but the book wasn't blue) that was about Walt Whitman. At that time I was unsure if that's what Ed was trying to bring to our attention. We would find out 8 days later that this wasn't the book.

As we were leaving, Ed came to me a final time and told me to hug his father, whom I had just met for the first time that morning. I told his dad, "Ed wants me to give you a hug" as I hugged him goodbye. It was very emotional for me, as I felt Ed was using me to give his dad one more hug from him. We now have a special bond that didn't exist before this trip and for which I'm forever grateful. I told my partner Tom, "It was really awesome taking a vacation with you and your late partner, Ed."

This journey serves as a perfect example of how signs, words, messages and symbols that a medium provides from a loved one may not be immediately apparent or obvious. You have to investigate them to make sense of them. There are reasons why a spirit gives these things to a medium to convey a message, and there is always a way to make a very personal confirmation.

Other Signs Confirmed One Week Later

Eight days later, the two unsolved mysteries of "the blue book" and the words "duke or duchess" would be solved. That's when Ed's father sent us a letter in the mail with some answers that surprised all of us. Over the dinner table, Tom started reading the letter:

> *"I think I may have a connection on the "Blue Book" and "Duke/Duchess." See what you think.*
>
> *First the book. Thinking about the story of Cornelia Clopton and her appearance 50 years later in her former house, I know that somewhere I had that story by a local newspaper columnist which I clipped from the paper.*
>
> *I was looking around downstairs when I happened to look through a book in which I had stuck some things years ago. This book had been sent to me by a cousin just after Ed died. (This cousin had lost his 19 year old daughter some years earlier and it was her memorial bench there at the cemetery where we met [last week]).*

The book is a collection of stories recounting after-death contact and experiences by people who had lost loved ones. I also put in the book 4 accounts by my cousin of his encounters with his deceased daughter and I had been wondering where they might be.

This book was a life-saver for me at that time and I kept it close to me and read and re-read it constantly for 2 or 3 years. It brought me great comfort and was an emotional life preserver. It is standard size and of 350 pages. Front and back covers are blue, as well as the cover jacket."

I immediately jumped up and started running upstairs, leaving Tom sitting at the table calling to me, "What are you doing? Where are you going?" I had run upstairs to get the book I was reading and brought it back downstairs. Tom said, "Ed's dad sent a photo of the front cover of the book," and as he laid it down on the table I put the VERY SAME BOOK (copyright 1995) on the kitchen table at the same time!! Tom and I looked at each other in surprise.

Tom looked back down at the letter and continued reading it. "The title of the book is "HELLO FROM HEAVEN." Above the title are the words "Have you been contacted by a loved one who has died?" I enclose a photo." This was indeed the blue book Ed wanted his father to find! How did the confirmation come to pass?

The weekend before we traveled to central Virginia to meet Ed's father I felt an urge to stop by the local Border's Bookstore. Obviously, Ed was pushing me to go in there. I went in, just wanting to browse and had nothing in mind. Of course, I went over to the area that had ghost stories and books about communication with those who have passed. For some reason (which I now know was Ed pushing me), I picked up and purchased the same book that Ed's father had Hello from Heaven by Bill and Judy Guggenheim.

In fact, I brought the book with me on our trip to Virginia, but left it at the hotel when we met Ed's father. This was a true confirmation that it was the book Ed wanted his dad to read again and the title "Hello from Heaven" was an obvious greeting from Ed to his dad, Tom and I! Amazing!

Ed's father's letter next addressed the message of "duke and duchess" that I received and that we couldn't figure out during our visit. Ed's dad's letter continued:

> *"The impression Rob received of "Duke" or "Duchess" may well be "Count" or "Countess.*
>
> *If you recall during our tour around town, I stopped very briefly in front of a home across from the beautiful mansion called "Villa Maria." I mentioned, off-handedly, that it was once the residence of Countess Raffalovich and that Eleanor Roosevelt had visited here. None of us seemed to catch it at the time and we moved quickly on in our whirlwind tour of the town.*
>
> *My sister has a recipe for Countess Raffalovich's spaghetti and ever since I moved back to town in 1998, my sister has invited us over every 2 or 3 months to have a spaghetti dinner. "Countess Raffalovich's spaghetti" has long been a common expression among us.*
>
> *About 2 weeks ago, my sister was exulting over her new dishwasher and I said "Well, you will have to fix the Countess Raffalovich's spaghetti and invite me over so we can dirty some dishes."*

Ed's dad went on to say how I was likely interpreting "duchess" as "countess" which makes perfect sense. So, what does it mean? It means that Ed's spirit was there when his dad was talking about being invited over for "Countess Raffalovich's spaghetti."

Sometimes the signs that spirits give us may not be obvious, but usually over a short period of time, they become apparent, just as every sign that Ed's spirit gave me made sense. This was one of the most incredible adventures in mediumship I have experienced. Ed's spirit is very strong and has been communicating with me for years since Tom and I met.

The most rewarding aspect of this is that after 15 years, these signs and proof that Ed is still around his family has finally brought Ed's father peace and brought peace to Tom as well. I'm thankful to have Tom as a partner, and I'm thankful to know Ed so well, even though I never met him when he was alive on Earth. I've grown to know and love him in spirit.

The following story occurred before that adventure. In 2010 we met an old friend of Ed's for lunch, and Ed joined us there, too.

Spirit Joins Us for Lunch

In 2010, we met Robert L., an old friend of Ed's who was visiting from central Virginia. Ed's spirit also joined us for lunch.

Robert relayed several stories of visits from Ed's spirit. He said that Ed's spirit has visited his house several times in the past 12 years. Our lunch marked the first time that Robert and Tom were physically in the same room since Ed's services 12 years before.

At lunch, Robert and Tom started talking about Ed. I started getting my tell-tale headache in the back left side of my head, indicating a ghost or spirit is around. Ed's spirit suddenly filled me with feelings of his love and friendship for Tom and Robert.

Although I couldn't see him, I sensed him sitting in the empty chair next to Robert (Tom and I were sitting on the other side of the table). Ed conveyed a couple of messages to me. He said he "screwed up," and did something that led to his passing in his 30s. He said to tell Robert and Tom to stop talking about the funeral and wake and talk about the "funny things" they used to do together. Ed filled me with so much emotion that I teared up. That happens if you're a sensitive medium - you feel the emotions.

As we were served lunch, Ed said "Tell them I love 'em" and then he told me to ask them about a "small silver car." I had no idea what that meant. When I mentioned it, Tom recalled that Ed had a small silver car that he used to put his landscaping tools and even a lawnmower in! That silver car was Ed's way of proving to all of us that he was indeed sitting with us over lunch that day.

CHAPTER 5: LESSONS LEARNED FROM TALKING WITH THE DEAD

Some Misconceptions That Need Clearing Up

There are a number of misconceptions about death and the afterlife that people have as a result of various rules established by religions. One such misconception involves infants who pass away.

The book *Hello from Heaven*, had a story of a woman whose infant daughter died. The woman who lost her baby was a church-going woman she told the authors that because her infant daughter didn't get baptized, she feared the spirit of the baby was doomed to eternal hell! Wrong. Baptism is a man-made practice.

I was a Catholic, so understand where that doctrine came from. However, the church was wrong to say that if you're not baptized you go to hell and don't experience peace in the afterlife. Think about how cruel that sounds if you love an infant, dog, cat, or person who has never been baptized. Infants don't go to "hell."

In 2011, an infant girl came through to me with messages for her family. This was a girl who was too young to know language before she died. I'll explain how infant spirits can communicate in a later chapter. However, this infant gave me words, pictures and messages for her surviving relatives and told me she's with relatives on the other side.

I confirmed all of the things the infant girl told me. She also assured me that she was in a beautiful place in the afterlife. She was with family members. She was at peace and wanted her parents to know.

There are many misconceptions religions have taught people that need to be corrected. These misconceptions do nothing for those left behind except cause agony, grief, and unnecessary pain. Where these religions get these ideas, I don't know. What I do know is that they are wrong. People can now take comfort in knowing their deceased infants can cross over and need not be "baptized."

Checklist of What Happens After Death

Following is a short checklist of answers from people who passed, to some major questions I've been asked over time:

1. You don't need to be baptized to go into the light and a peaceful place in the afterlife.

2. Dogs, cats, and horses have intelligence and souls. All animals have souls and go into the light in the afterlife. Religions that teach that pets do not go to the afterlife are wrong. My late puppy and many other dogs have come to me. I've confirmed things about their lives with their owners.

3. People who are sick in life, mentally or physically, or have lost a limb, sight, hearing, etc. are made whole in the afterlife. People who had Alzheimer's disease are freed of it in the afterlife. Mentally and physically handicapped people are made whole. Mental illnesses disappear once someone passes away, enabling the deceased to understand their behavior on Earth.

4. People who are gay cross into the light. Religions are wrong. Love is love and love is not evil. Spirits of many gay people have communicated with me and many others. Similarly, people who are tattooed and eat shrimp go to cross into the light (same passage in Leviticus). It's about energy, not man-made religions.

5. People who commit suicide go into the light. Some choose to linger behind on Earth in an effort to reconcile taking their lives, and then cross over. An awakening occurs when they die, and they feel grief, agony, and guilt for taking their own lives. They work to forgive themselves and learn on the other side. Eventually, they move into the light and achieve peace.

6. People don't appear in the afterlife as they did in the last stages of their life on Earth. People appear in spirit in the way they were most comfortable in life. For example, people who die at 92 may appear in the 40s or 50s, when they thought they looked best. My own father passed at 79 and appeared to me as a 30-something year old. Infants who die may also appear as full-grown adults, because in spirit they are adults who came to Earth as an infant.

Choosing Happiness on Earth

Everyone goes through trials in life, although some seem unjustified and unfair. I know people with illnesses that could make them depressed or mad at the world, but they are the most loving, wonderful, optimistic people. They radiate love. They know the secret of life. Spirits want us to choose to be happy and optimistic.

I have experienced time in my own life where I should have been miserable - hiding who I was and being scared and unable to live the way that would make me happy. I realize that was wrong and I wasted a lot of time, but I enjoyed every day. I also came out of that time appreciating life. At one point I lived off student loans while getting my degree in meteorology, eating tuna fish and Ramen noodles while working two part-time jobs that barely paid my rent and car insurance. But I was thankful I was able to do it.

I know people who have great jobs, houses and don't worry about paying bills, yet they are miserable. They're healthy for the most part, but can't find much positive about their lives. Some haven't found love, others found it and left it behind, and just dwell on what they don't have, instead of appreciating what they do have. There are a lot of people who live paycheck to paycheck, who choose what bills to pay, decide on food or electricity, but somehow they remain optimistic. It's all how you look at life.

Someone told me, "I can't be as happy as you. It's not natural." Well, it is natural. You can choose to be thankful for a sunrise, or a hot cup of coffee, or getting green lights on your commute, or having a dog or cat to hug, or a book or TV show you liked. Find the simple things in life that make you happy and recognize them.

The bottom line is you can choose to be happy, or choose to be miserable. We all have obstacles. Wherever the difficulties are, whether in career, health, family, education, residence or other factors in life, we need to dwell on what is good. I choose to be happy. You can, too. It will not only improve YOUR life, but people will want to be around you much more.

People who Hate, Abuse, or Discriminate, and Forgiveness

Hatred in any form is wrong. I've learned a lot about what happens to entities after they pass if they hated, discriminated or abused others. Treatment of others affects what happens to us and others in the afterlife.

Hatred and intolerance in any form hurts both the victim and the perpetrator. Mental or physical abuse is a serious offense. Mentally ill people may not have the ability to recognize that their actions are wrong while they're alive, but they gain an instant understanding of how wrong their abusive actions were once they pass; then they beg for forgiveness and understanding because they were unable to help themselves.

Sometimes, people use religion to promote hate and intolerance. In Maryland, some churches rallied hard against marriage equality in 2012 and some "religious people" said all people are not equal. The pastors and their congregants who believe that are 100 percent wrong and they will find that out once they pass away. That, however, is too late.

Creating laws that also prevent equal treatment is one way that our political system promotes discrimination. Regardless of one's religious background or beliefs, you must know in your heart that intolerance and treating other people as being "less of a human" is wrong.

In the 1800s, the U.S. abolished slavery. In the 1900s, women and African-American citizens finally got the right to vote. In the 1960s, couples of mixed race were finally able to marry. Progress has been slow in reversing discrimination, but discrimination still very much exists.

Bullying is a serious problem today in our schools and over the Internet. Children and adults are bullied because they are fat, thin, black, white, Hispanic, Asian, gay, straight, atheist, religious, rich, poor and for many other reasons. Whatever the reason, discrimination and bullying is wrong and those who do it will have to atone for it in the afterlife.

Similarly, people using religion to promote hatred and intolerance are no better. The Bible says to treat all with love, no exceptions. In fact, there are 10 times more Biblical references against adulterers and divorcees than gay people and recommendations that divorcees be stoned! How ridiculous.

If you're reading this and are a social conservative, it may be hard to swallow. However, you need to step outside yourself, put your religion aside and look at the situation. Not everyone follows your faith and we are all equal. If you despise someone based on your belief in God, what kind of God are you worshipping? The God that I grew up with in the Catholic Church was one of love - before the church got involved in politics and started using money to fight gay marriage. Then they lost their way from a "loving God." All people are God's children, no exceptions.

If you follow any religion or don't follow one at all, you should love and accept everyone. Forgive others. Help others. Don't hate, separate or abuse others. If you do, you'll be stuck on Earth for awhile until you atone for your bad behavior. If you don't believe me, once you've passed, you will immediately know that your behavior was wrong.

Abusive People

Abusive people are a different story than those who choose to hate and discriminate. Some people who are mentally and physically abusive to others have a mental illness. Once they pass, however, I believe the errors of their ways become clear to them and they are sorry for their abuses.

I went to a cemetery with a friend whose father was buried there. His father was abusive to my friend both mentally and physically. When I drove into the cemetery with my friend and we got to the place close to his father's grave, I heard his father say to me "Please tell him that I'm so sorry. I was not in control of my actions, but I'm aware how wrong they are now. Please ask him to forgive me."

44

My friend's father needed that forgiveness to move on; and often that's the hardest part for those left on Earth who were the victims. Since then, I've met a lot of people who had an abusive parent who has passed, and I tell them the same thing. Their late parent now understands that the abuse they did was wrong and they are seeking forgiveness. Their minds are clear on the other side.

In one instance, a spirit in a higher realm told me he could see a spirit in a lower realm, but could not interact with them.

How Do the Dead See the Abuse or Hatred They Have Caused?

Once our physical bodies die, the energy that is our soul either stays on Earth or crosses into the light. For people who were abusive, hateful, or discriminatory, and committed bad acts to those still living, their entities can live trapped as Earth-bound ghosts because they need forgiveness for what they have done.

I believe that once a soul leaves its physical body there's an immediate awakening of bad behavior committed when the person was alive. It's like a curtain is lifted from their eyes and their bad behavior or mental illness is gone on the other side. My experiences have shown they finally have clear thinking and immediately see that their actions were wrong and hurtful.

People who passed told me how sorry they are for mistreating others. This includes parents and others who were mentally or physically abusive, murderers, alcoholics, thieves, drug addicts, suicide victims, people who hated others because of their race, gender, sexuality, religion, weight, disability, or anything else. In all instances that I have seen, these souls are very sorry for being hateful or abusive to themselves or others. So what do they need to help them leave Earth and move into the light? Forgiveness.

These ghosts and spirits to get messages across to those left alive on Earth to not treat others as they did. Unfortunately, ghosts and spirits usually can't get that message across to the living. So, what happens? People on Earth make the same hateful, stupid mistakes as those who have passed and learned way too late.

45

Why Not Forgiving a Dead Person is Detrimental to Your Health

The paramount lesson is to forgive anyone who has wronged you in any way. Of course, people who were physically, mentally, and sexually abused usually can't forgive those who committed the offense if the offender is still living. That's understandable. However, once the offender physically dies, their ghost is going to remain Earth-bound, seeking forgiveness for the horrible things they did when they were alive.

How does that affect you? Ghosts that linger in your home spread negative energy. Ghosts use negative energy to power up and interact with the living through visible appearances, noisemaking, moving things, etc. Because ghosts use negative energy to "energize," they also emanate it. And they give it off to the living people in the house, causing arguments, tension, and bad emotions.

If a ghost who was haunting a home where people are living finally crosses into the light, the people in the home will notice that the tension eases between them. You may have also seen this same thing on various episodes of the "Ghost Hunters" television show.

The bottom line is that if you have an Earth-bound ghost in your home that you know may be seeking forgiveness for something they did to you, find it in your heart to really forgive them and tell them to move into the light. Once the ghost is gone, you'll immediately feel better emotionally.

What Can We Do to Acknowledge the Dead's Message in Our Lives?

Here are a few simple rules to help make you a better person: (1) Don't be hateful toward others. (2) Treat others as you would like them to treat you. (3) Put yourself in others' shoes- How would you feel dealing with abuse and hatred? (4) Stop yourself and stop others from hateful behavior. (5) If you don't understand and have adverse feelings toward someone, reach out to them and try to understand. Get to know them. Change your ways. We are all on Earth to share it, live together, and help each other.

What if You Continue Discriminating and Hating?

You'll have to atone for discrimination and hatefulness in any form after you pass, according to my communications with the dead. One relative of mine was trapped on Earth for over 20 years begging for forgiveness from my own mother. For an entity to remain on Earth is like what hell is like. Think of all the ghost hunting programs that pick up audio saying, "Help me." Those entities want forgiveness and help crossing into the light. The ones that don't get it are trapped here for eternity and experience a living hell. Don't let it happen to you!

Spirits Want You to Celebrate Their Lives

After we lose a loved one, it is easy to grieve and dwell on the fact that they are no longer here in the physical sense. However, spirits don't want us to dwell on their passing. I believe they want us to celebrate their lives. They live on, and they are around us from time to time after death.

So how do you honor their memories and learn to live life again? Here's how I did it. In November 2010, on what would have been my dad's birthday (he passed in 2008), I read Vince Flynn's *Extreme Measures* paperback because he was one of dad's favorite authors. I felt certain that as I read it (even through my thoughts) my dad could hear it, as if I'm reading it to him. My dad is also with me when I write letters (he always did), or enjoy Dunkin' Donuts coffee (as he did).

If you've lost a loved one, do something that they used to enjoy doing, and tell them you're doing it for them as a remembrance. They would want us to remember them in a good way, and doing something they would enjoy is a nice tribute to them.

CHAPTER 6: POLTERGIESTS

Poltergeists are actually not ghosts. A poltergeist is supposed to be a restless, angry, disturbed, or unhappy ghost. However, the Physics and Mediums Web site (www.psychics.co.uk/) from the United Kingdom says, that "Most paranormal researchers believe that poltergeists are not ghosts at all, but manifestations of unconscious mental upset, usually in children or teenagers." The Web site explains objects are moved or noises are created as a result of a troubled teen's psychic energy. Moving an object with your mind is called "psychokinesis."

In October 2010, I received confirmation that a teenager was responsible for poltergeist-like activity. I attended the New Life convention in Maryland and met a woman who shared her story. The woman told me two supernatural experiences in her life. She is married to a military man who came back from Iraq. She said that some of the men in his company did not come back, at least in the living, breathing sense of the word. They died in battle overseas. She went on to say that some of those men returned in the spiritual sense around her and her husband, who had since retired from the military. She said her husband is very skeptical that the dead soldiers are around, but she senses them. I told her that if she and her husband do not want the soldiers visiting, they should tell them to move into the light and they are "relieved of duty."

She didn't understand why they would be breaking many glasses in their home. She sensed that they're loyal to her husband, their commander in the service, but doesn't know why they would do something to upset him.

She mentioned she and her husband have a daughter. I asked if the daughter was a teenager... Why? Because teens dealing with conflicting emotions, stress, or angst can create poltergeist activities, such as breaking glasses. Through more conversation, I learned that the activity ceased when her daughter wasn't in the house. So, the breaking glasses were not caused by spirits. They were broken by her daughter's emotional energy. Therapy is recommended for teenagers with extreme emotional issues, and once teens receive help, the poltergeist-like activity should wane.

CHAPTER 7: PROTECTING YOURSELF FROM GHOSTS

Ghosts who stay behind are beings of negative energy. That doesn't mean that ghosts are bad or negative entities, however. In fact, some ghosts are content to be trapped on Earth because they chose to be. Some ghosts are people who lived in a home they loved and don't want to leave it.

Some entities choose to remain Earth-bound because they may have unfinished business, and they think that by hanging around they can influence others or communicate with them to accomplish something (although that rarely, if ever, happens). Others are attached to a place, memory, or sense of belonging. There are an infinite number of reasons why a soul could choose to remain behind on Earth as a ghost, but they need to be reminded that their loved ones are waiting for them on the other side. Basically, they need to cross over into the light.

Earth-bound ghosts use our negative emotions to "power up." Emotions such as fear, anxiety, nervousness, hatred, and selfishness are all things that help a ghost manifest and make its presence known. Ghosts are basically made up of and thrive on negative emotions, and this has nothing to do with their personality or behavior as an Earth-bound entity.

For example, when I visited the Marietta Mansion in Maryland, very gracious ghost of a woman (and former owner) made me feel welcome in her home. Because she's Earth-bound, she draws off negative emotional energy, yet she was not a negative entity.

Because Earth-bound ghosts use negative energy to power up, they also (if unknowingly) emit negative energy, which can lead to emotional problems between you and the people you live with. It's a circular pattern that's difficult to escape because the ghost creates negative emotions around the living and the living react with negative emotions toward others living in the house. That emotion powers the ghost, and the cycle repeats itself. The solution is to clear the house of any ghosts and clear the emotional atmosphere of your home.

Sensing a Ghost

In July 2011, I attended one of Medium Barb Mallon's sessions in Virginia. Periodically, Barb hosts open sessions for up to 35 people at a time, where she tunes into spirits and gives readings for people within the room.

During this particular session I was blocked from receiving most messages from spirits because of a dark entity in the room. This was a ghost that was impressed upon a young woman in the room, like a heavy feeling, and the woman appeared very uncomfortable.

When Barb Mallon told her that the spirit of a male friend (not the dark entity) was coming through to give her messages, the woman broke down into tears.

During Barb's reading, my friend Troy (who is also a developing medium and very sensitive) was writing down his feelings from the darkness surrounding the young woman. He and I felt the exact same things. I was also writing down what I was sensing. We both sensed that the young woman was dealing with deep depression (something that Barb Mallon would later tell us she also sensed). We all sensed that the young woman had dabbled in some dark things, too.

As for the dark entity, something happened that had never happened before - I saw a clear image of this male figure and sketched it out immediately. The man was wearing ankle-high shoes with big buckles on them, similar to what you would think Pilgrims might have worn. He was covered by a black robe that hung down to the top of his shoes and a black hood on his head. His face was obscured and in darkness, except for green eyes that shone out from the blackness.

He told me that he lived in 1648. History notes that Jamestown, Virginia, was settled in 1607, while Pilgrims arrived in Massachusetts in 1620. Given that we were at a seminar in northern Virginia, it would make sense that this man was from the Jamestown settlement, about 150 miles south.

He was a dark entity because he was angry. Anger is a "dark" emotion. He was angered because he said that he died too young. As a result, he wasn't ready to cross over, so he stayed behind as an Earth-bound ghost. He showed me what looked like a black stalk of wheat with flames coming out of the side of it. That could indicate that he was a farmer and that his farm caught fire. Perhaps that's how he died. I'm unsure.

So why had he impressed himself upon this young woman? The answer lies in her mental state. She was depressed and appeared emotionally unsettled. Ghosts thrive on negative energy and are attracted to it, so, this ghost was attracted to that woman's mental state, because she acted as a power source for him. The ghost told me that he was drawn to her because she either lives or lived somewhere close to where he died. Her negative emotions acted like a beacon to the entity that pulled him toward her.

Negativity and ghosts can become a vicious cycle. If you're a negative thinker, Earth-bound ghosts (negative energy) can be drawn to you and use you as a power source. In turn, a ghost generates more negative energy to keep you depressed and pessimistic. It's a vicious cycle you need to seek help to break.

When Troy and I compared notes after the event, he told me that he experienced pain in his chest, just as I did. We also realized we both had pressure headaches on the top, left side of our heads. That meant the ghost was sharing the pain of his passing with both Troy and me. I couldn't get a reading on what kind of death those pains were associated with, however.

After the event I talked with Barb Mallon and decided to show the girl the sketch I made of the dark entity that I sensed is attached to her. She broke down in tears and said, "That is exactly the man I saw in my house and my backyard, and who keeps following me."

I told her that she needs to rid herself of negative emotions in order to free herself from this ghost. She needs to focus on positive things in life (that's good advice for anyone). I told her to write down one thing that makes her happy or thankful for each day. She also needed to set some ground rules with the entity.

Setting Some Ground Rules

If you're not consulting someone that knows how to help Earth-bound ghosts cross over, you can at least set some ground rules.

First, you need to take a stand with the entity and tell them that this is "your house now." They don't belong there anymore. They may have owned this house at one time, but they have passed away, and you rightfully, legally own the home. Tell them to go into the light and join their relatives awaiting them on the other side. Portals of light can be found at funeral homes, hospitals, or even cemeteries, and they should cross over and achieve the peace they deserve.

If you can't get them to cross over, contact your local paranormal society or group, and tell them that you need an entity removed from your home. It's important to remember that a ghost was once a living, breathing person who chose to stay behind for some reason and is now trapped here because they don't know enough to cross into the light or even look for it. Some ghosts don't understand that they're dead and need to be told. Speak to the entity as if you were speaking to a living person in front of you.

While you're waiting for the entity to be removed, you may want to try the following to protect yourself, your family, and your pets (who are very sensitive to ghosts) from a ghost in your home. Imagine yourself and your family surrounded by God's white light of protection, kind of like a shield. This white light can be pictured around you whenever you go into a house that you may think is haunted or anywhere at any time. Usually when I get ready for sleep, I envision a white light around me and my family.

On the nights that I forget to do it, I tend to wake up at 2:30 a.m. or 3 a.m., when the spirits seem to be most active. The white light of protection really seems to work. I believe that James Van Praagh and Maryann Winkowski mention it in their books. Give it a try!

There are many other things you can do to protect yourself and rid yourself of negative energies and ghosts. Contact local paranormal groups, such as local ghost hunters, or learned mediums, like Barb Mallon (www.barbmallon.com), who can provide guidance.

Preventing a Ghost From Following You

If you are moving out of a home that you know has a ghost that dwells in it, you need to make sure that the ghost does not follow you to your new home.

Margaret Ehrlich, the manager of Inspired Ghost Trackers of Maryland, gave the following good advice, "I don't think a ghost will follow you, but just to be on the safe side, make sure you tell them that they can't follow you. Tell them they are not welcome to accompany you and they must stay in the home. If they do follow you then call your local paranormal group for help." Another member of the Inspired Ghost Trackers suggested lighting a candle to absorb all of the negative energy (ghosts are negative energy) and then discard it in the trash.

My understanding is that ghosts typically stay at a place that was comfortable and familiar to them when they were alive. As Margaret mentioned, it's important to tell a ghost not to follow you and to stay put. Better yet, tell them to move into the light.

Some other things you can do that may prevent a ghost from following you to your new home include sprinkling sea salt just outside the front door to block them from leaving.

You should also picture yourself surrounded by white light and positive energy. Positive energy acts as a block to a ghost's negative energy. Finally, as you are leaving the home for the last time, think positive thoughts. Remember, ghosts feed off negative energy, so don't give them anything to cling to.

CHAPTER 8: SPIRITS, ANNIVERSARY DATES AND HOLIDAYS

Birthdays, anniversaries and holidays are occasions that spirits use to acknowledge their presence. In this chapter you'll read about a spirit who made her presence known two years in a row on a certain date to prove it was her - although it took me two years to realize it. A spirit may come through on an anniversary or birthday that relates to them or someone they are connected to and are usually around during holidays when family members gather together.

Medium Barb Mallon of Chantilly, Virginia, often sees balloons or flowers to signify such an event. She'll ask the person she's reading if there's a birthday or anniversary around the date she's giving the reading and there always is one.

In a later chapter, you'll read how my late puppy Buzz visited another medium on what would have been his sixth birthday. Even dogs and cats can recognize birthdays and anniversaries and try to convey messages.

The birthday or anniversary can be related to the person or pet that passed away or to the person the message is intended for, or someone connected to them. It's just another way of the spirit confirming personal knowledge that a medium, for example, would have no prior knowledge of.

Mediumship brings pieces of a puzzle that you have to make sense of, and sometimes that occurs over time. In one case, my friend Kathy's mother's spirit visited me three years in a row, during a certain week each year.

A Mother Returns

My friend Kathy lives in Florida, and her late mother Pat (whom I've never met) came to me in 2009 when I was taking a shower. On March 1, 2010, Pat had another set of messages to relay to her daughter Kathy, and she decided to again use the water energy to convey them to me while I was in the shower again!

Here's what I told Kathy: "Hi Kathy, last night your mom Pat came to me again, and it was in the shower again, too. Funny, everyone else seems to talk to me when I'm not in the shower, but I guess your mom knows I'm cornered there, so I have to listen.

Your mom told me that she loves her 'TV chair' and still enjoys it from time to time when she's checking in on you. I have no idea what it looks like, only that it was her "spot." Can you explain? She told me she's around when you're mowing grass on a sit-down mower, and that you should be careful around them."

Pat's message was "Kathy should check out the lawnmower because there may be a problem with it." She also mentioned the last book she was reading and to think of her whenever Kathy saw Minnie Mouse.

Kathy wrote me back and confirmed several of the things, while unable to explain a couple of others. She told me that she had purchased the two chairs in front of the television a couple of months before her mother died, and her mother loved her new chair. She also noted that she enjoyed going to Disneyworld with her mother, thus, the Minnie Mouse connection.

Kathy was startled most by the lawnmower message. She sometimes mows lawns for her employer. That week when she was mowing the lawn, the sit down mower was making weird noises and she was thinking that she should get it checked. After the message, she quickly got it repaired.

A Mother Provides a Vacation Message a Year Later

On March 8, 2011, one year and one day after she last came to me, my friend Kathy's mother gave me more messages. There are some interesting facets of Kathy's mother's visits over the last two years. One is that they were both around the same week, and another is that they were both when I was in the shower surrounded by water.

Getting messages from Kathy's mother within 7 days of each other in 2 separate years was her way of proving it was her.

It's not unusual to get messages in the shower because spirits can use water energy and because it's a place where you can relax and open your mind. There are no distractions like television or radio, and no one talking with you. Relaxation is an important part of receiving messages.

On March 9, 2011, I emailed Kathy and told her that her mom gave me some messages, but I didn't know what they meant. Although I've known Kathy 16 years, I had never met, nor talked with her mother Pat (I only lived in the same state for a short time).

Pat's spirit told me that Kathy needs to take a vacation in November 2011. She specifically said "November." She also mentioned that if Kathy does go on vacation, she may finally meet a nice guy, but needs to be open to it.

One thing that struck me funny was that Kathy's mom appeared to me as a "cartoon image" of herself, like she was trying to be funny. Kathy is still having a difficult time dealing with her mom's passing, years later. I figured out that Pat was trying to tell Kathy to lighten up, laugh more and enjoy life.

Typically, spirits will come to the living they always want to be remembered. Usually, they appear younger than when they passed, appearing at a time they were most comfortable with in life.

Kathy's mom also gave me other signs, but Kathy wasn't yet able to confirm their meaning. The one thing she did confirm was surprising enough. She and her friend have already planned a vacation in November, probably the week of Thanksgiving!

Kathy said that her mom "could be right about the laughing at life more. It has been a rough few months and that is probably what she is talking about as well."

On March 31, I emailed Kathy and asked her what the significance of the week of March 1st is to her mother. I guess I should not have been surprised when she told me that her mother's birthday was March 4th! That is totally understandable. It was another cool confirmation that it was she doing the communicating.

A Brother Visits at Thanksgiving

Holidays are one time that spirits come back to be with family members. Just like the living gather on holidays, those who passed still want to be with them as they celebrate.

On Thanksgiving night, 2010, my friend Lynn's brother Michael visited me in spirit with a bunch of messages for her. Why Thanksgiving? Because it's the time that the family was gathered and Michael wanted Lynn to know that he was there with all of them. (Michael passed long before I ever met Lynn, and I've never seen a photo of him). Following are the messages and Lynn's answers:

- *Michael told me that that he was with your mom and dad having Thanksgiving.*
- *He said something about "sharing your eyes." - Like your eye color.*
Lynn confirmed that Michael had the same eye color as both she and her dad, providing proof that it was him.

- *Michael said that you should "try to not be so impatient."*
Lynn said that she just spoken those very words aloud to herself the previous day when she was driving. That confirmed that Michael was in the car with her that day.

- *He also said he loves what you've done & you look "Fabulous!"*
- *He said he loves you very much and mom and dad send their love, too.*
- *He wants you to have a wonderful Thanksgiving, and know that he and your (late) parents are all with you at the dinner table.*

Because Thanksgiving is the family holiday, it was even more important to Lynn to hear that Michael was with her and her family on that day.

The bottom line is that spirits (not ghosts) will often come back during anniversaries, birthdays, holidays or some date that is important to them or someone that is still alive. This is their way of giving an obvious sign that they are trying to communicate.

CHAPTER 9: CEMETERIES, BATTLEFIELDS AND HAUNTINGS

Every day I learn more about how ghosts and spirits behave and why and where they appear. Over the last year I've realized that their energies are still drawn to their physical remains.

Typically, ghosts and spirits don't linger in cemeteries. They usually haunt or frequent places that were familiar to them during their lives on Earth. Think about it. If you were trapped on Earth as a ghost (under your own choosing) would you linger at the grave where your body is buried or stay in a house you lived in and enjoyed? The exception is ghosts who linger where they died or were murdered.

In the case of battlefields (there are many Civil War battlefields along the U.S. east coast), ghosts or spirits may be drawn there because they may be buried there, they may have died there in battle, or because of the emotional energy they expended during the time of war. I'll explain about battlefields shortly, but I grouped them with cemeteries because both have bodies buried in them.

In my first book I told of a former roommate's late mother who appeared in my home as a dark entity because her ashes were in the house. My puppy Buzz, who passed in 2005 and whose ashes we have in our house, makes appearances from time to time. Their energies are drawn back to the remains of their physical forms. That brings me to the topic of haunted cemeteries.

Cemetery Experiences

Ghosts typically haunt places where they lived or enjoyed during their time on Earth. They don't typically dwell in cemeteries. However, if a living person is anxious or fearful while walking through a cemetery, they could provide energy needed for a ghost (drawn to the remnants of its previous physical form) to manifest. Spirits (who crossed into the light), can manifest in cemeteries from positive emotional energy such as love and hope, if one of their living relatives goes to visit a grave.

I did have one experience in 2007, where a ghost manifested in a cemetery. It was in the Christ Church Burial Ground at Arch Street between 4th and 5th Streets in Philadelphia, Pennsylvania.

According to the Web site www.christchurchphila.org, that cemetery is the final resting place of over 4,000 people including Benjamin Franklin. Four others who signed the Declaration of Independence are also buried there, in addition to military heroes from the Revolutionary War and Civil War.

While visiting Philadelphia, we walked through the burial ground. In the back left-hand corner in I saw a man dressed in 18th century clothing just standing there. I knew he was not alive, because he more resembled whitish ectoplasm. He disappeared after a minute. I couldn't figure out why a ghost would appear in a cemetery, but now I know. He was drawn to his remains and "powered up" when living people with emotional energy came close by.

If you go to a cemetery and see or experience an Earth-bound ghost or a spirit who has crossed, you're probably enabling them to make their presence known with your emotional energy.

During a talk I gave in 2010, I learned of a spirit appearing at a cemetery. A woman in the audience told me that she laid flowers at her son's grave (he was killed in the military), and she took several photos of the gravestone all newly decorated. She said two pole-like white mists appeared in a picture. She realized that they were the legs of her son, who was standing there watching her! That's an experience of love powering up a spirit to appear at a gravesite.

A Loved One Visits at Her Grave Site

The weekend of Saturday, July 24, 2010, would have been Tom's grandmother Grace's 100th birthday. She passed in 2006 and her presence remains strongly today, just as the presence of many people's late grandparents remain around them. Grandma has been tossing pennies to Tom since she passed.

On July 24, we drove to Virginia with our dogs and visited Grace's grave.

Not surprisingly, I got my tell-tale headache indicating there was a spirit or ghost present. Grandma had passed into the light, and the love we brought helped call her to the cemetery. While there, Grandma's spirit gave me several messages. She told me how she would go out in the backyard kitchen (separate from the house) and bring ice cream to Tom when he stayed there as a child. He confirmed that.

Grandma Grace was really funny. I only knew her about 6 months before she passed and 5 of those she spent in a nursing home. She had a good wit and was loved by many people. She did a lot of sewing for people, and was a good cook, always canning food.

While we were at the cemetery, I sensed some other spirits that were able to "power up." One spirit was leaning against a tree, another sitting on his gravestone.

Next time you visit a cemetery, whether to pay tribute to a loved one, pray for them, investigate historical markers, or even to just walk through it, you may not be alone, depending on what emotional energy you give off.

Battlefield Hauntings

Now I'd like to address battlefields. When people are killed suddenly, they sometimes don't realize they're actually dead. Sudden deaths can produce a mental blackout period and the soul awakens separated from the body.

Sometimes the soul doesn't realize he or she has been killed and lingers trying to make contact with the living. Other times, they'll see their dead physical body and move into the light. Sometimes the emotional energy of the death or deaths in the case of a battlefield, will linger. Such is the case in many of the Civil War battlefields.

Gettysburg, Pennsylvania, is well-known for residual hauntings, where battle charges can be seen at night by the ghostly men who participated in them during the Civil War.

Residual hauntings occur when the same thing happens over and over and there's no ability to converse with the living. It's like a movie being rewound and replayed over and over.

There are also reports of intelligent haunts at Gettysburg, where ghosts will interact and communicate with the living by sounds, movement, or other signs.

If you've lost a loved one in a war or conflict, speak to them and tell them that if they are stuck on Earth as a ghost, they need to move into the light and cross over. If you've dreamt about them, it means that they've already crossed over and they're at peace.

The Wilderness Battlefield, Orange, Virginia

In March 2011, we took a trip to central Virginia and stayed in the town of Orange. Although I was aware that Civil War battlefields peppered Virginia, I didn't realize we would be driving right through the middle of one until the energy became overwhelming.

Fortunately, I was in the passenger seat. As soon as we entered the area, my head was filled with thoughts of sadness, anxiety, and nervousness. When I started getting these feelings, I wondered what was going on. When I looked up from the book I was reading, I saw that we were driving through a forested area on Route 20 in central Virginia and learned then that we were driving through the "Wilderness Battlefield."

The Wilderness Battlefield is located near Orange, Virginia. It's about 15 miles from Fredericksburg and on what is now state Route 20. Generals Lee and Grant battled there for the first time on May 5 and 6, 1864. That two-day battle brought 26,000 deaths and was Grant's first movement toward Appomattox.

Once we got past the battlefield area, the energy began to wane and my head cleared. If you go to a battlefield and sense there are some Earth-bound ghosts (intelligent haunts), please instruct them to move into the light so they can finally achieve peace. The visitor's bureau Web site says "Orange County is rich in Civil War history." I can vouch for that.

CHAPTER 10: SLOW DEATH EXPERIENCES, FUNERAL HOMES, WAKES

While we're on the subject of cemeteries, this is a good time to address people going to their own wakes and funerals. First, however, I need to talk about what happens when someone is in failing health and near death.

When Someone is Slowly Failing

Death is a strange thing because it's a transitional moment where we transform from physical beings of beings of energy. It is also a time when we sometimes get a look at the afterlife, before we're entirely part of it. Sometimes people on the brink of death come back and forth between worlds. Some even leave their bodies for a time and come back to them.

There are many reports of people dying in a hospital bed but they are aware of happenings to people they know outside the hospital. This is possible because people in the state near death sometimes leave their bodies. As an entity composed of energy, they are drawn to the ones they love, wherever they may be on earth. Love acts as a beacon for that traveling soul.

For example, if your cousin in another state announces to her mother that she's pregnant, your father who lay dying in a hospital hundreds of miles away may tell you at the same time that your cousin is pregnant. His spirit likely left his body to visit his sister (your cousin's mother) to hear the announcement before you did.

People's energy sometimes leaves their bodies before death, whether to intentionally come in and out of the physical body, or to leave it just before a sudden accident.

Leaving the Body With a Message

In May 2011, I was talking about my abilities with a hair stylist named Sherry. She told me she understood about our energy temporarily leaving our bodies, also known as astral projection.

She mentioned that her father was slowly dying in a hospice and she visited him daily. One day, like many before, the caregivers told Sherry that she should go home now and that her dad would be okay overnight. Sherry said that she went home and felt his energy around her. He had temporarily left his body and followed her home. She told him that it was okay to pass and not linger for her or her mother.

"Within ten minutes of my telling him it was okay to cross over, I got a phone call from the hospice that my father had passed," Sherry said. She was amazed but said that she knew he had indeed heard her give her "okay" to move on.

Relatives Ready to Guide to the Afterlife

Whether someone dies quickly from a car accident, or gunshot, or other type of accident or their health is slowly declining in a nursing home, hospital, or house, they will likely be visited by relatives or friends who have passed.

Oftentimes, patients dying slowly in a hospital will tell the living that they've seen someone in the room who has passed. This is likely because the deceased relatives or friends appear to reassure the dying person that everything will be alright and that they can pass to achieve peace. They come to help alleviate the fear of dying and to guide them to cross over. After a visit from a spirit, the person who is dying usually gains a sense of peace.

The dying person might opt to stay behind for a little while to watch his/her memorial service or may cross over immediately. My own father stayed during the week of his services, and I watched him cross into the light later at the cemetery. Others may stay behind and become trapped until someone tells them to go into the light. For some reason, Earth-bound ghosts seem to forget how to cross over if they linger too long - they must be reminded.

In sudden death, although spirits of relatives or friends may appear to try and help someone cross over, the newly deceased person's soul may be so disoriented that they may not pay attention to those trying to help him.

Such was the case of a man involved in a car accident in Elkridge, Maryland. Several years ago, when I drove past the site of an accident that happened earlier that day, I sensed his energy standing at the scene. Later in the week, his energy was gone, so spirits of his loved ones likely appeared and led him into the light.

Sherry the hairstylist told me she had an out-of-body experience during an accident, and came back to it. She said that she was involved in a car accident and lost a lot of blood. She told me that she remembers leaving her body and experiencing a warm, peaceful feeling. She said that she felt as if she were floating.

She explained that she was given a blood transfusion at the hospital, and the doctors and nursing staff brought her back as her energy re-entered her body. She told me, "I was envious of my dad's passing because it was so beautiful and peaceful (on the other side)." There are many accounts of people leaving their physical bodies just before an accident and later returning to them when they're recovering in the hospital.

Visit During a Slow Death Experience

During the weeks of June 12 and 19, 2011, my friend Maureen's father, who was nicknamed "Bumpy," was slowly fading in a hospital. His wife had passed more than 20 years before.

On Sunday, June 19, 2011, I was taking a shower and Maureen's mother's spirit came to me with a message that surprised me. I sent Maureen a text message immediately that said, "I heard from your mom tonight - I was just in the shower and she said

> *"tell Mo dad will be fine. I'm waiting (for him to cross over). She said something about a little black?? (yes, I wrote 2 question marks) dog named Pierre. Does that mean anything to you?"*

Maureen's text message back to me at 10:09 p.m. EDT that night said:
> *"OMG! (Oh, my God) I am going 2 call U OK?"*

64

She called. She was overwhelmed. Pierre was a black poodle that was her dog during childhood. I don't recall ever meeting Pierre or hearing about him. Pierre had been on the other side for more than 30 years. Maureen was totally amazed, as I was. Shortly after that phone call, Maureen sent me a photo of Pierre on my cell phone, just as her mother's spirit described him to me. I was in awe.

I also asked Maureen if her dad had seen his wife's (Maureen's mother) spirit in the hospital room. She confirmed that her dad did see her mother's spirit in the hospital room. Maureen also told me during the week that her dad said that he had gone "to Heaven" and came back during the week.

On June 24, Maureen sent me a text message that said *"Bumpy went to Heaven to be with Mom and Pierre."*

Visiting Funerals and Wakes

In my first book I recounted that my own father passed during the writing of that book and came to his own funeral and wake. He gave me very specific signs that helped me prove he was there.

People who pass away often go to their wakes or funerals, and sometimes both. Others will cross over immediately when they die and may come back to "check in" and see who came to pay their respects. The entities that stick around might also cause issues for their loved ones left behind while they're waiting for all the services to end.

By issues, I mean they can affect the electricity in the house of their spouse or family. My dad's energy stayed around my mother's house that week and caused the lights in the house to go on and off, electrical sockets to short out, and some new light bulbs to not work. Once Dad crossed over after his funeral, those things stopped.

Even today, his spirit comes back from time to time to play with my mother's hallway light. She's had it checked by an electrician and there's nothing wrong with it. Now my mother just stands in the hallway and says out loud, "Okay, cut it out!" and it stops.

Messages Come Through at a Wake

In June 2010, our friend Cynthia's step dad Wesley passed away. He was 88 and suffered from memory loss and dementia. As Tom and I were driving to the wake, Wesley came to me with a number of messages, many of which took me and Cynthia by surprise.

The first one was "Cindy Lou." I heard that name over and over, and I didn't know who that was. It turned out that's what he called Cynthia. I was blown away by that! The next message was about one of her brothers and she understood what it meant. The third thing he told me was what happened as he passed. He had bleeding on the brain, and he told me that he "heard a pop" in his head, and the next thing he knew, he (his spirit) was standing up in the hospital while the doctors were working on him.

He stayed for a brief time (about 2 days) and was then ready to cross. He said he felt no pain and didn't remember any. Spirits typically don't remember any pain associated with passing.

He told me that he was transitioning to the other side (he was still at his wake) and he could think clearly now, like a great fog has been lifted from his brain. Because he passed, he was freed of the dementia and made whole - thoughts now clear. He mentioned how he had missed "Honey Bun" (his wife), who is hospitalized in a different care center, but would now be watching over her.

The last thing he said was to "thank Cindy Lou" for all of the love, care and attention she provided to him, especially since he fell ill. When I told these things to Cynthia it brought her to tears, but happy tears. She said, "You said that exactly as my dad would say it." She was very comforted to know he's okay on the other side and at peace.

This was the second wake I had been to in 2010. The first wake I went to that year also surprised me.

Another Communication at a Wake

The month before Cynthia's step dad's wake we attended a wake for Tony, one of Tom's former high school teachers. Like Cynthia's step dad, I never knew this man when he was alive. Before going to this wake, I hadn't been to a funeral home since August 2008 and I didn't know what to expect.

As soon as we walked in the door, I got my tell-tale headache, indicating there was a ghost or spirit present. In fact, I know there were at least two there (there were two wakes going on). One wake was for an older woman and the other was for Tony.

While waiting to sign the guest book I kept hearing "Maura," or "Mara," or a female "M" name. I determined the name belonged to an older woman for someone being waked in the other room.

Once we entered the crowded and noisy room full of people talking, laughing, and carrying on, I entered and stood in the back of the room. I didn't know anyone, and my partner knew many people (former classmates and teachers).

I stood with my back to the wall while talking with my father-in-law, and I felt a finger poke me in the back. I turned around and no one was there. I was poked again, and I knew it was "Tony" playing around to let me know he was there.

Ghosts and spirits know who can sense them. Sensitive people are like a beacon that attracts entities. The entities know they'll be able to communicate with the sensitive person.

As I continued to stand at the back of the room, I sensed that Tony's spirit was poking his head into small groups of people conversing. He was turning his head as if he were trying to hear what they were saying about him. It was pretty amusing to watch.

Tony's spirit really seemed to be enjoying the crowd of people there to honor him. When I later told my partner about Tony's goofy behavior, he said, "That's exactly the kind of thing that Tony would do! He was a prankster in life. He loved to joke around."

When a couple of young men walked by me (there were a lot of younger men aged 20 or so), Tony told me which ones were his sons. I knew going in that there four sons, but Tony pointed out three. One was a taller man wearing tan slacks and a checkered button-down shirt. Another son was dressed in a dark suit. The third son was standing in the hallway wearing a black shirt.

Tony kept nudging me to tell his son dressed all in black that he was still here and was enjoying seeing who came to honor him. I was reluctant to do that, however, because of the very conservative religious beliefs of the family. If you have abilities as a medium, it's important to know who you can and cannot give messages.

The religion that Tony's family subscribes to teaches (erroneously) that mediums "talk to the devil." It's really frustrating to me, because I could've provided some comfort to the family. I heard and "saw" Tony, and know that he was grateful for the show of love and support during his wake.

When I came home after the wake, I posted some of the encounter on my book's blog. The next day, my mother-in-law wrote the following email to me, because she personally knew Tony:

> *Hi Rob- I just read your note about Tony's appearance. You were right re: him poking you. He liked to play pranks on people. His sister said at the funeral how he would take Jelly drops and insert the middle with pepper and give them to her to eat and then laugh when she spit them out.*
>
> *You didn't see his fourth son as he is autistic and was out in the hallway. He had on a brown shirt. He wrote a letter to his father that was read by his mother at the service re: how he was glad that his father was now with his brother.*

That email provided another confirmation Tony was there and trying to communicate with his family.

It's important to realize that as much as those who have departed want to communicate with someone, mediums that get the messages need to be careful to not anger those left behind. Mediums must be mindful of other's religious beliefs. Some religions erroneously believe that messages mediums get from ghosts and spirits come "from the devil or are evil." I personally find that ridiculous because messages from those who passed can offer comfort to those left behind.

I did have one instance, however, where I made that mistake. I told someone that her father came through and he even provided me with the woman's husband's name and other things that were correct, but the woman's religious beliefs instead made her angry and react in a very nasty way toward me.

Yes, I was only trying to offer comfort and pass a message. You have to be careful whom you tell. If you do get messages for someone, don't just pass them along if you think the living person may be hostile to you and not believe you.

Regardless, the point of this chapter is that most of us do come back or hang around for our wake and funeral just to see who showed up. Next time you're attending a funeral or a wake, just know that the person who passed away is likely watching everyone and everything happening during their services from a different perspective.

CHAPTER 11: WHAT ABOUT SUICIDES AND MURDERS

People who commit suicide do pass into the light. Some take longer than others to transition because of the amount of time it takes to develop an awareness that it was wrong to take their own life. Usually, the realization happens pretty quickly after the person dies. This is similar to those who mistreated others during their time on Earth; once they pass, there's a quick awakening that their behavior toward others on Earth was bad.

Upon realization that what they've done is wrong, those who commit suicide work on getting the forgiveness they need from the people they hurt emotionally. They also learn how to forgive themselves. Then they can move into the light. People who commit suicide do not go to "hell," that's a religious fallacy.

If you know a suicide victim, tell them that you forgive them and that they should move into the light to achieve peace. Being trapped as an Earth-bound ghost is as torturous as living in an isolation cell, where communications with loved ones are cut off and you're unable to help yourself. Forgiveness and direction from the living can enable suicide victims to achieve peace in the light.

Murder victims sometimes stay behind because they don't know that they're dead. Sometimes they linger and forget they need to cross over. If you're ghost hunting and come across an entity who was murdered, it is important to tell them to go into the light. In this chapter you'll read about an investigation I took part in with my friend Troy, who is also a developing medium. We had no knowledge of anything that had transpired in a private residence and were able to piece together the events of a double murder.

A Medium's Messages from Suicide Victims

I asked my friend and learned medium, Barb Mallon, about messages that she has received from suicide victims. She is an evidential medium who brings forth identifying pieces of information from a spirit person first and then any messages they may have.

Barb Mallon has been featured on numerous radio shows and has appeared on television, including on The Discovery Channel. She conducts readings for clients locally and all over the world. She does in-person and phone readings and gives seminars. She can be reached through her Web site www.barbmallon.com.

Barb told me the following about messages she's received from victims of suicide:

I have received two common messages from suicide victims. The first message is that they are okay and not in some state of limbo, but that they are 'not off the hook,' and have to still learn the lessons they came here to learn. They equate their still having something to learn to not being able to graduate with a class.

For example, it's like messing around during your last year of high school so you don't have the grades to graduate. Instead of graduating with your class in the more celebratory way, you have to go to summer school and get your diploma in the mail instead. It's not horrible, but it's still work and it's not as fulfilling as completing your 'life courses' as you should and 'graduating with your class.'

The second message I get is that they are not in some 'hell,' but that said, they DO see and experience what they did and how they made others feel, as we all will. I was under the impression that suicide victims see what they've done as if reviewing their life in a movie setting and explained this to a mom who lost her son to suicide. Later, I was awakened in the middle of the night to the same gentleman who said bluntly that I didn't quite get it right. He said they see and FEEL what they've done to others. This can be most rewarding, or can put a spirit person through a kind of "hell" if they weren't such a good person, or they caused extreme pain by intentionally leaving the Earth plane. In all cases, I'm told that the suicide victim is met and helped with love by their guides and loved ones on the other side.

Following are encounters with spirits of those who committed suicide.

Message Received at a Convention

On October 9, 2010, I attended the "New Life Convention" in College Park, Maryland, with medium Barb Mallon.

A woman I'll call "Mary" came to our table and explained her sister passed recently. Mary's sister had been a troubled teen. Suddenly I sensed Mary's sister's spirit standing there.

The spirit of the girl told me to tell Mary that "it wasn't Mary's fault that she took her own life." When I told Mary what her sister's spirit said, Mary said she felt guilty and thought she should've helped her sister more. Mary's sister's spirit was very forceful in trying to have me convince Mary that it was her time to go. The spirit said, "I chose to ignore Mary's outreach, and I knew Mary was a "rock" for me, but I had to make my own mistakes (that took her life)."

At the end of the brief, emotional reading, Mary's sister's spirit told me to hug Mary for her, which I did. We both teared up. Mary said that she "knew that she was supposed to come to my table for some reason," and she was brought over. Her late sister had a message for her and that was the only way she could get it to Mary.

I was so emotionally drained afterward that I had to sit down. It was unexpected (as such experiences usually are) and wonderful, in that it brought some peace to the woman who stopped by.

The message for anyone who knows a friend or loved one who takes their own life is that YOU should never feel guilty. That person chose to do that act. They do regret it in the afterlife, and I believe they will always try to assure the living that they're okay.

Medium Communicates With Spirit of a Suicide

In 2011, I enjoyed an evening performance of medium Lisa Williams, an amazing woman. I first saw her on a television show carried by Lifetime. In 2010 she had two television specials on the Style network.

Lisa Williams is a medium who understands the power of her gift. She receives messages with amazing clarity and was right on target all night.

One of the most astounding readings she gave was about a murder-suicide. She explained that a man had killed his wife, then killed himself. Both appeared in spirit beside her with messages for their grown daughter, who was in the audience. The daughter identified herself after Lisa gave more information. It was amazing. Lisa explained that the father and mother were on "different levels" in the afterlife, although they could speak with each other. The details she provided were just amazing. The father was seeking forgiveness for taking his wife's life and then his own. The daughter in the audience had forgiven him.

For more information about Lisa Williams, visit her Web site: www.lisawilliamsmedium.com.

Receiving Messages While on the Computer

Sometimes when I'm working on the computer, my mind is relaxed and I'm receptive to messages. In March 2010 I was emailing a friend and business colleague named Jill, whom I have never met in person. Jill lives on the other side of the U.S. from me, and I met her through my full-time job.

I told Jill about the first book I wrote *Ghosts and Spirits: Insights from a Medium.* She told me that she bought the book and hadn't yet read it when she emailed me on March 25. It was on that day that I learned that Jill had lost her best friend John to suicide months before. She was still reeling over the loss.

Following is our email exchange which allowed John to connect to me and give Jill some messages to let her know that he's okay and at peace.

From: Jill   Sent: March 25

Hi Rob, [the book] is in my briefcase, and I'm in the process of moving. But funny to get this timing wise, my best friend died (suicide) and it has been a rough journey.

When I got the book my first thought was a way of finding John. I haven't read it, as I was at the memorial last weekend and packing to move.

Have you ever heard anything about anyone who chose to leave this place? I sure would like to connect with John and tell him I love him, of course he knows it's okay, we were best friends, and had many discussions about his situation. Still very sad and I have a lot of unresolved feelings. I can't get my head around it.

The book is going to go on my nightstand as a first read in my new house once I get over there, I am really looking forward to exploring it. Sorry, that was a bit heavy of a reply, wasn't it?!
Jill

From: Rob   Sent: March 30

Hi Jill - I just found your email from last week in my inbox. I am so, so sorry about John. My deepest sympathies. As a matter of fact, I've heard a lot from people who have chosen to take their own lives.

Last week an old classmate from elementary school called when she read about the book. I haven't heard from her in 25 years... but she tracked me down. Her 19 year old son took his own life and has come back over and over to her. He's also at peace - but realized that it was a mistake. That's typically what happens, spirits have an awakening when they reach the other side.

It's important to talk with John (he can hear you). Tell him that you want him to cross into the light and find peace. Look for signs. I'm getting a headache in the back of my head, and I believe he's with me.

Did he drive a dark colored car, like a red car?
He's showing me medications or some kind of drugs. Is that how he passed?

74

I get the image of a starfish, too, like he liked walking on the beach. Do you know what that means?

He's showing me a classroom. Did you meet in a classroom? I'm unsure what this means, unless it's that he could have learned from you and others on how to overcome his obstacles.

He's passed into the light. He can see you from where he is... he's okay. He realizes that he made a mistake but couldn't handle life here anymore. He was weak. He should've talked with you and some others more, he said.

Who is the person who is associated with him that starts with "K"?
He's around that person, too. Is that a brother or sister, or other relative?

Were you able to get a memento from his belongings after he passed? He'd like that to happen.

WOW. That's what I got. Let me know if this makes any sense to you.
Rob

Jill's response came shortly after I sent the email with the messages that John gave me:

From: Jill   Sent: March 30

Rob - He had a dark Italian sports car that he loved, before he got into financial issues.

He couldn't get medications, because he was against a wall financially and had no insurance. He suffocated himself with helium in bed. We met 23 years ago right before his father passed away. We were best friends, he adored his mother unconditionally.

He doesn't have any siblings. I have his mother's kilt he wants me to wear at Christmas in her honor. And I got packages of photos and mementos 2 days after he died. He labeled everything, a history of his life, and his heritage. He called me the morning of, because he wanted to talk to someone who loved him. I am very sad, I miss him so much I just cry thinking about it. I understand where he was at. Yes he was weak, but very, very proud. He wouldn't come live with us, he had too much pride.

I feel guilty I didn't do more to stop him. I hope he's with his mom and dad, because they loved each other so much. I used to call him every morning at 5:30. I still reach for the phone on my way to work. Then I get mad because he's not there. All of these emotions to go through. He's one of the kindest people I know, with a huge heart full of love for my daughters.

I think the classroom image is him reminding me to get those girls through college. He paved the way for that to happen, and a goal he was determined they both reach.

One of the pictures he sent me is of him and two buddies walking on the beach in Ireland. I included it in the CD I made for his memorial. Whew.

I wrote back to Jill, surprised that she was able to confirm so many of the signs John gave me that morning:

From: Rob   Sent: March 30

Jill - Wow. That's a lot of signs from John and you were able to confirm them quickly, which is amazing.
1) The dark colored sports car.
2) The picture at the beach with his friends in Ireland is the sign! He kept showing me a starfish and a beach.
3) The other people he's around are likely his parents on the other side.
4) The image of the medications now makes sense, he couldn't afford them.

5) I'm glad that you have boxes of mementos and the kilt. Those are all important to him, and are important that you have them.

6) The classroom scene makes sense, too - that he wanted to make sure your daughters go through college, especially since you said it was a goal.

- Do you know who the "K" person is that he told me?
He doesn't want you to get mad at the fact that he's not here. He wants you to still "call him" at 5:30 a.m. every day, but without the phone. Just talk to him. He's listening. Just know that he's around whenever you want to talk with and he is at peace - and he's checking in! I hope this brings you some comfort, Jill!
Rob

Jill thought about the "K" sound of the person John was trying to communicate and wrote me back later. Sometimes it takes awhile for someone to connect names, pictures or words that mediums receive. Fortunately, Jill came up with the answer quickly.

From: Jill   Sent: March 30

I bet I know exactly who that is! Although not a "K" I bet it is B. Ricci (pronounced "Rikki"), and imagine he's grinning with a Gin and Tonic in his hand :-) Yeah, I listen for him in the wind... he'll know what that means.

A little more than a week later, John returned with more messages for Jill and urged me to send her an email. I did. Here are our emails:

From: Rob   Sent: April 8

Good morning, Jill! I wanted to drop you a note because I was thinking about John this morning for some reason. I felt a gentle tugging on my left arm and felt as if it were him. It made me think that he would tug on your arm from time to time.

He said that he appreciates your talking to him. He can hear you and he's smiling. He said he's content now, and he's able to watch over everyone at the same time from where he is. He tells me that where he is, is like sitting on a patio chair watching the sunrise. He's tugging at my arm again. He says to send his love and that he'd like you to wear his watch once in awhile. Maybe you can tell me what this means.

He's really a strong personality. He's got a firm or smug smile right now. :) Let me know what you think. Hope you're having a good morning. John says hello and sends his love.

Rob

Jill wrote back and provided more confirmation of John's signs and messages.

From: Jill   Sent: March 30

Hi Rob, I didn't get it when you kept saying to talk to John, but you mentioned in the book to talk out loud. Right after he died I would sit out on my porch and cry and yell at him and verbally spew my heart out. I'd stopped, but feeling better now, will talk out loud (good stuff John). I still cry, but it's okay, so long as he knows just because I love him and miss talking with him so much my heart aches.

About the watch. That is unbelievable! Well, actually believable it is, wow! Yes, he sent me a family heirloom pocket watch his father wore. It is on a long gold chain in my jewelry box. He asked me to wear it, or have Meagan wear it once in a while if she didn't think it was too dorky. Incredibly sentimental for him.

Did I send you the link of the video we made for his memorial? A lot of pictures of his mom in there as he adored her and his father. I really hope they're together. Jill

78

Hi Jill - Wow. I just watched the entire video. How beautiful. He was so loved and still is, it's obvious. I loved what you wrote on it, too. I sat here (at home) and cried through the entire thing. I also saw that beach photo! WOW. Really hit home with me.

What a handsome guy. When I saw him, he showed me his younger self. It's very interesting because when we pass, we choose how we're going to appear to others. Spirits typically pick a time when they were most happy with themselves, or when they were younger. My dad also did that. He came to me and showed me how he looked when he was in his 30s. You'll see his photo in the book.

That's so cool about the watch! I'm so glad that he's able to connect through me to give you messages. And he thanks you for talking out loud to him again. :)

Thanks for giving me permission to share these stories with others. I feel that each story gives others comfort and hope that their loved ones are safe and happy on the other side. A big hug to you from me and John!

Rob

Helping Suicide Victims

The bottom line is that people who commit suicide DO pass into the light. Sometimes they may linger on Earth for awhile to work through their own guilt. They need to learn to forgive themselves for being weak, and they usually ask for forgiveness from the living.

What's important for those of us who are left behind is to forgive them. It's also important to talk with those victims of suicide and tell them that they need to pass into the light if they haven't done so.

Despite what some religions may tell us, people who commit suicide do not go to "hell." "Hell" is actually what being trapped on Earth is, as a ghost. Imagine being separated from your loved ones (who are in the light) and unable to communicate with others who are living. It's like being in an isolation cell. That's how we used to punish prisoners here on Earth. Being a ghost is just like being in an isolated prison cell.

Remember, ghosts linger in places they were familiar with in life. If the suicide victim comes through in a place they didn't know (or to a medium), the person has most likely crossed into the light. Further, if you dream about someone, that's an indication that they have crossed into the light.

A Murder Investigation

Following is an investigation I participated in with Inspired Ghost Trackers and my friend Troy (who is also a developing medium). Both Troy and I were unaware of why we were investigating a private residence and what had transpired there. It was only after Troy and I went through the house that Margaret, the group leader, explained what had happened there.

INVESTIGATION: Private Home Investigation
DATE: August 17, 2011, 7 p.m. EDT
PARTICIPANTS: Inspired Ghost Trackers of Odenton, Maryland. Investigators: Margaret, Ronda, Julie; Mediums: Rob, Troy

Several investigators met Troy and me outside of a private home. Margaret Ehrlich, the founder of Inspired, was aware of details of what had occurred within the home but did not share them with Troy or me. She wanted to find out if what we sensed matched the accounts of what happened.

Margaret entered the home and asked if we were coming in. Troy and I were looking at the left side of the home and told her, "No, we want to check outside of the house first." We were both drawn to the left side of the house and walked over there. We looked at a side (painted white) door and felt a lot of energy there. Troy sensed it had a strong energy attached to it, a sense of urgency.

At the corner of the house, we saw three large electrical boxes, and wondered if they were generating electrical fields that were giving us feelings. Electrical fields can generate nausea or uncomfortable feelings, as if someone is watching you. So, Ronda checked the boxes with an EVP meter and found no electrical energy being emitted. We made a note of it and walked into the backyard.

Troy suddenly said that his hands and forearms felt as if they were weighted down, heavy as if they were bandaged or wrapped. Ronda was recording all of Troy's sensations on her hand-held recorder. We would later learn that two women who were murdered in the house and were bound at the wrist.

We continued walking into the backyard, and I was drawn to the back left side of the yard near the neighbor's fence. I sensed that there was a dog buried in the backyard near the tree/shrub line, either on the property I was standing on, or in the neighbor's yard. I then heard a voice in my head saying "Leave my dog alone." Troy also sensed a dog buried, also most likely in the neighbor's yard.

As we walked around the right side of the house, I felt nothing, but Troy seemed to have an experience. He felt an energy that seemed very different than what he had sensed on the other side of the house. This energy felt "uncomfortable" and dark. He would later learn that a dark shadow figure had been reported in the bedrooms on the other side of that wall of the house.

We then entered the house through the front door. I went first. Margaret said, "Which way do you want to go?" I told her I was drawn to the basement and the rooms on the left side of the home, so I went down. The first room on the left was a small throughway where the furnace was located. As soon as I stepped over the threshold, I experienced vertigo. My head was spinning. Something traumatic happened there. There was fear, anxiety. I walked into the next room, which was set up like a daycare room. Troy was right behind me and asked, "Did you feel that?" He asked about dizziness, light-headedness, just as I experienced. Margaret also experienced dizziness in the furnace room.

As we entered the daycare room the feeling stopped. We described it as "walking in and out of a bubble of emotional energy."

In the other room we experienced some temperature changes. Both Troy and I sensed a woman. It would be a little later in the evening that we realized that we were sensing two different women. Troy was sensing a younger woman in her 30s, and I was sensing a woman in her 60s or so. I later learned she was 70 years old. We later learned both were murdered in the home.

Ronda, Julie, and Margaret were operating thermometers to look for temperature changes and digital recorders and EVP meters to pick up any voices from entities.

Troy was getting strong signals from the younger woman. She seemed to be slight of build with longer brown hair, wearing what appeared to be a simple white dress. During the experience he could sense her reaching out, as if remembering a moment of anguish. Troy said he sensed a female giving him a name that began with the letter "M." Margaret later told us that related to one of the woman killed in the home was a girl named "Marissa."

I sensed the older woman was frail-looking and thin. She was also afraid and seemed somewhat subservient [but that could have been fear of the murderer]. I sensed that she had dark brown hair, and I saw her standing at a counter preparing food. She was chopping up yellow, green, and white vegetables. That was later confirmed when I learned she managed a bar where she served drinks and food.

I walked to the back of the room and the air got heavy and thick, as if walking through shoulder-high deep water. There was a lot of emotional energy there. Ronda noted a small temperature drop of a degree or two, and we explained it by the fan in the room. Troy walked in the back, and he also felt the heaviness. He then returned to the front of the room and stood near the large white door that led out to the carport. He was still puzzled by the energy that seemed to be attached to that door.

It was the <u>same</u> energy Troy felt while standing outside on the carport (on the other side of the door) earlier. He said that it felt like a powerful memory had been impressed on the door, as if a male had been opening and closing it with a sense of urgency.

We walked back through the furnace room to the downstairs open "living room" and kitchen area. Troy and I didn't sense anything in the basement kitchen, as if it had been cleaned of any energy.

We walked into the two back bedrooms downstairs, and I thought that whatever female ghost was there was in the mother's room. The son's room next door didn't provide me with any feelings. As Troy walked into the first bedroom, he was drawn to the bottom right-hand side of a four-posted bed. He suddenly felt an overwhelming sense of emotional energy as if a female had been crying in that spot during a moment of panic and/or despair. We later learned one of the current residents had been awakened several times by a shadow figure at the foot of the bed, pulling on her covers and on her foot.

Before moving into the house, the residents had actually requested replacement of the carpet in that room because of a large, "bleached out spot." They said that it looked as if someone had tried to clean something out of the carpet in the exact spot where Troy had experienced the strong wave of emotion and where they had experienced the dark shadow figure.

As we left the bedrooms, I wanted to go back to the daycare room. I told Margaret I sensed an all-female energy in the house. I would later learn this was because there were two women murdered in the home. They were both still there as Earth-bound ghosts.

We again walked through the furnace room, and again Troy and I experienced vertigo until we got through to the other room. That emotional energy was overwhelming in the furnace area, and we suspect it was where one or both of the women put up a fight. Margaret later confirmed that one of the women was still alive and struggling with her attacker as he struggled with her near the furnace room. The emotional imprint of her energy was still there and that's what we felt.

83

After reviewing the evidence and photos from the second Inspired Ghost Trackers investigation, the face of one of the women appeared behind an orb in the furnace room. The photo appears in this chapter.

After re-entering the day care room, Troy sensed a male figure behind him and said the female ghost wanted to stay away from the male figure. I also had the sense of a male, but only saw a shape behind Troy. Troy and I we both thought the figure could be of the woman's late husband but couldn't get a read on him. We thought the woman may have been in an abusive relationship and she was afraid of her husband. We couldn't tell if the man was an intelligent or residual energy and were trying to understand.

Meanwhile, Ronda and I were standing beside each other and got goose bumps. Interestingly enough, the goose bumps appeared on my left arm and Ronda's right arm- indicating to us that the female ghost, whom I would later learn was the older woman (murder victim) was standing between us. The female ghost was afraid.

Immediately, Ronda and I asked her questions: What is your name? What are you doing here? Why didn't you move on? Can you look for the light and go into it? What are you afraid of? Of course, we didn't get audible answers but hoped something would come through on the digital recorder.

Then, not knowing if the male shape was a ghost or projection, Troy took action. He told the male entity to leave and go in the backyard. We would later figure out that the male figure may have been a projection of the man who murdered both women, or the elder woman's late husband.

We then explored the second level of the home and were only drawn to the front right corner of the house. That was the same corner Troy and I were drawn to on the outside when we first arrived. We were a floor above the white door (that we felt energy on which led from the day care room connecting to the outside carport.

Before we returned downstairs, at the top of the stairs I felt like someone was trying to push me. I also got a strong headache on the front left side of my forehead. I was wondering if one of the women was hit in the head and pushed down the stairs. I later learned that both women had been shot repeatedly, and the younger woman also had been beaten on the head. That was the strong headache I felt in the front of my head.

When we returned to the day care room for the final time, we tried to get the ghosts of the two women to cross over, but they would not yet go. One last message I received unnerved me.

I asked Margaret to turn off the recorder for a minute, as I was hesitant to reveal the message I received. I asked Margaret if a woman was sexually assaulted in the house. Margaret told me that it was true.

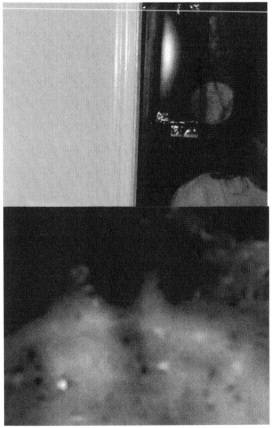

(CAPTION: Top- the original photo in the daycare room that includes the orb in the furnace room. Bottom: Close up of the orb showing the face. Credit: Inspired Ghost Trackers, Odenton, Md.)

It was also at that point that Troy reported having the sense of a woman being violently struck on the side of her head (back handed) by a male just inside the door at the base of the steps. After the investigation I checked a newspaper account and confirmed that the younger woman had been sexually assaulted with a pistol.

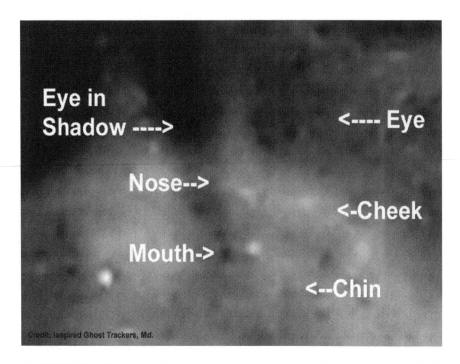

(CAPTION: The face is clearly a woman's and the woman's left eye is very clear here- right eye in shadow. Nose is visible. Mouth is visible. Credit: Inspired Ghost Trackers, Odenton, Md.)

Both Troy and I researched newspaper accounts after the experience. I learned that a county judge convicted the murderer of three counts of capital murder and five related charges in the slaying of his landlady and a younger relative in 2002.

The murderer had rented the basement apartment from elder woman. The elder woman was shot, beaten and killed in the basement apartment. The younger woman was shot, beaten and sexually molested and near death. The murderer brought both women through a back door and around to the carport. We later determined that the killer left an energy imprint on that white door facing the carport that both Troy and I picked up on.

The two women's bodies were later found in the trunk of the younger woman's car, parked in a nearby apartment parking lot.

The Inspired Ghost Trackers returned to the house two days later to help cross over both female ghosts. Ronda said that she did not think they wanted to leave.

Both ghosts have been in that house for ten years and were trying to get the attention of the current homeowners. It seems as if they two women were watching over the new inhabitants to keep them safe from men like the one that murdered them and do not want to cross into the light.

CHAPTER 12: COMMUNICATIONS FROM NON-SPEAKERS

Just because a spirit did not or could not communicate in a spoken language when he or she was alive, doesn't mean he or she can't convey messages of words or pictures as a spirit (not an Earth-bound ghost). That's because once our entities become spirits, we develop a great awakening and knowledge.

Once people pass, everyone becomes whole again on the other side and develops an understanding of life, death, and communications. People who were sick in life are free of their sickness as spirits in the light. People who had lost limbs during their time on Earth are made whole again as spirits. How is this possible? It's important to know that our souls are "recycled."

We have all lived before as someone else and we will all likely come back again. Those who we are connected to in this life are the souls that we were connected to in a previous life. This is why people have memories of a previous life that they can't explain. Sometimes they're even able to validate and prove they lived a life before through research.

One example is that of a little boy named James Leininger who was six years old in 2004. He was obsessed with airplanes and even at the age of three, he knew what "pre-flight checks" and drop tanks on aircraft, yet he had not been exposed to that kind of information. His parents at first didn't believe he was drawing from memories of a past life.

It turns out that James had memories from a 21-year-old Navy fighter pilot who was shot down by Japanese artillery during World War II over the Pacific. The little boy was even taken to meet the surviving family members of the pilot who, were astounded with memories only the pilot could have had. At age of three, some children are still struggling to speak, yet this child knew the different parts of a World War II aircraft. Possible? Yes, but unlikely.

The book containing this story is *Soul Survivor* by Bruce and Andrea Leininger, published by Grand Central Publishing in 2009. It's an incredible story and proof that some of us were here before.

Why do souls keep returning? We come back to learn more lessons. So how does coming back help us communicate if we die in this life as an infant? Because in addition to developing an awareness of communication on the other side, most of us in one past life or another likely reached adulthood and had an understanding of language and communications.

That's some background on how and why infants and animals that pass away are able to communicate with the living. Following is a personal example of an infant who passed and communicated with me, followed by examples of animals in the next chapter.

An Infant Communicates With Me

On April 30, 2011, I attended a medium event hosted by Barb Mallon. I referenced Barb in the previous chapter. Barb was giving readings over the two-hour session for the 40 people in the audience and providing some amazing messages (For telephone or in-person readings, contact Barb Mallon at Barbmallon.com).

During the session an infant came to me. I wrote all of the things down that she told me, and then after Barb's event, I read them aloud to the audience.

The baby girl (likely 2-3 months old) spoke with me telepathically using words and pictures as if I were speaking with an adult. She told me that she was a little girl who died in a crib. She told me SIDS (sudden infant death syndrome) or a heart defect may have been the cause of death.

She said that she's buried in a nice cemetery under a big tree, surrounded by lots of beautiful green grass, and she likes to run around in the grass. She then showed me a colored Easter egg. That indicated to me that she likely passed in the springtime.

She told me to tell her parents that she's okay. She showed me that she was happy, smiling and is at peace. She kept saying, "Tell mommy and daddy that I'm fine." She showed me that she was with her grandparents or great-grandparents in the afterlife, and that she was also with a scruffy, little brown dog! She also mentioned that she has a surviving brother.

As I was conveying the messages, the amount of love and emotion I felt was overwhelming. I choked up and was actually brought to tears twice. This little girl felt the pain her parents were experiencing and wanted to tell them that she's truly okay.

When I finished, I looked up and a woman in the audience was also crying. The infant girl was connected/related to her. She identified herself after I finished, and said that the little girl belonged to her. I was stunned, too. The woman came up to me afterward and said that everything made perfect sense.

The woman confirmed all of the messages. The little girl's name was Autumn. She passed in the springtime in her crib. Her great grandparents had passed and the scruffy little brown dog who passed was "Taz." The surviving brother's name is Hunter.

She thanked me for the messages and told me she's been grieving for four years since Autumn's passing. We hugged a couple of times, and she appeared to have a great sense of relief and peace. This is the real benefit of being a medium and sharing messages from those who passed. It made it all worthwhile.

A Medium's Understanding of Non-Speakers Communication

Barb Mallon is a learned medium who lives in northern Virginia and has the ability to communicate with those who passed. Barb has also been a mentor to me and has become a good friend. I asked her to share how non-speakers like infants and animals communicate with her. Like Barb, I have received messages from dogs and infants who were unable to speak in life, but were able to convey messages in the afterlife.

90

This is what Barb told me: *"I've actually been made fun of by many on the Internet about communicating with a deceased animal.*
People have asked: "What do they do? Bark their message to you?" While that would actually be a wonderful thing to experience, that's not how it happens. Just like in life, animals communicate with their humans through emotion and even telepathy. Have you ever noticed how your dog knows when you're sick and sits by your feet? Or your cat cuddles up to you if you're sad or upset? They understand through their intuitiveness what's going on with you.

When they communicate from the other side, they will normally give feelings (illness or emotions), pictures or snapshots of memories they have (I may see the back of someone's legs which tells me the animal followed their human around constantly).

They will tell me if their human was in the room with them when they were put down by making me feel absolute comfort and love the warmth of their touch. This always makes me emotional as I think immediately of having to put down a few of our fur children, but at the same time, I feel from the animal a sense of going through the process with someone who loves them very much.

Many times, a spirit person will tell me an animal is with them and then I'll eventually link with the animal. Sometimes, the spirit person simply tells me things about the animal and I won't connect. I feel they are letting me know the animal is with them, is okay and they need to bring up other messages or information instead.

Linking to an animal is the same process as when I link and communicate with a human who didn't speak English. I'll get mainly pictures, symbols, and feelings and sometimes words that sound very close to a word I'm more familiar with.

As far as infants, depending on their age, I normally don't get much about them. This is because they don't have much life experience that can be validated, especially in the instance of a newborn or small baby. I've linked with many 2 year olds who will give me exuberant feelings of "mommy!" I've even seen them running around their parents trying to play with their jewelry or shoes, etc.

91

CHAPTER 13: SOME INSIGHTS ON ANIMALS

Dogs, Cats, Horses as Ghosts and Spirits

Dogs and cats are living embodiments of unconditional love. In Dr. Stanley Coren's book, *The Intelligence of Dogs*, I learned that a dog's intelligence can be likened to a five-year-old human child. Being a dog owner, I've noticed that some dogs are smarter than others. In fact, one article I read in 2011 said one border collie actually has a 2000-word vocabulary!

Dogs, cats, and horses have spirit energy and souls just like people. Anyone who says dogs, cats, and horses don't have souls or spirits is simply uninformed. I learned that even certain pet birds can come back and give messages.

Our pets are waiting for us on the other side when it's our time to pass. I've seen them on the other side, as have many, many mediums. There are also many stories about ghosts or spirits of dogs, cats and horses. For example, one book focuses entirely on *Ghost Dogs of the South*, authored by Randy Russell and Janet Barnett and published by John F. Blair Publishing of Winston-Salem, N.C.

Animals Sensing Ghosts and Spirits

Not only do Dogs, cats, horses and some birds have the ability to come to us as ghosts or spirits, but they are also able to hear and see ghosts and spirits when some humans cannot. These animals possess not only intelligence of a young human child, but also emotion and heightened senses.

I learned from Dr. Stanley Coren's books that dogs hear at higher frequencies than humans, which is likely where ghosts and spirits "talk." Think of how Electronic voice phenomena or EVPs of ghostly voices are picked up by digital audio recorders when people holding them cannot hear the entities speak.

Dogs can also see entities better than people, according to the book *Inside of a Dog* by Alexandra Horowitz (published by Scribner a division of Simon and Schuster, N.Y., N.Y. in 2009). Horowitz said that dogs have more rods than cones in their eyes than humans have. That means that they can see movement more easily than people can, although they do not see as many colors as people see.

Horowitz said that dogs see the world faster than humans do and see more of the world every second. She said that television doesn't keep a dog's attention because dogs see the images as individual frames with dark spaces in between, like a strobe light. Human eyes, however, don't see the dark screens between the moving images.

It is because of a dog's ability to see motion better than humans that enable them to spot the movement of a squirrel from afar (although they only see clearly up to about 75-100 feet away, according to Dr. Coren, DVM). This ability also lends itself to seeing the movement of ghosts and spirits, as well. Because of the different makeup of dogs' eyes, they are less able to recognize colors (most colors appear gray, except for yellows and blues).

During one of my promotional book events in 2010, I received a confirmation of this from a man and his cats. A man came up to me after my talk and told me that his cat would often stare at an area in his basement. He said that one time, a white mist (ectoplasm, apparently) came from the corner and the cat ran. Cats as well as dogs have a higher sensitivity to movement and can see ghosts and spirits. In that case, even the owner could see the ghost!

Dogs Sense a Dog Lover

Our close friend Sarah passed away after a battle with cancer in May 2010. The next night, our dogs heard and saw Sarah in our house.

It's always a shock when we lose someone we love, no matter how much we understand what happens after people pass. Sarah was a tremendous part of our lives for the last 5 years of her life. I met her and her husband at a dog event we immediately connected.

Over the years, we had grown to love Sarah so very much. Sarah volunteered for dog rescues, and she and her husband adopted five dogs. They even took in a sixth foster dog.

Sarah was very excited for us when we got married. When we told her about we were planning a small local reception, she volunteered to bake gourmet cupcakes for all our guests. She baked for weeks! The cupcakes were such a hit that there were only two left after the reception, and people were still talking about them even a year later.

Just 6 months before she passed, Sarah went to the doctor to check a stomach ache and learned she had stage four cancer. She had been asymptomatic. It was a shock, but she never gave up hope. That was Sarah. She was the kindest, most loving, happy, optimistic person and always had a smile, a hug, and a kiss for us. I always looked forward to her emails every week asking for SNOW, even in July! Sarah LOVED snow. Well, during the winter of 2009-2010, I "gave" her two blizzards and record snow fell in the area. She was ecstatic, and always wanted more snow. She made me laugh when it came to my forecasts and the weather.

On the Sunday before her passing, we attended Sarah's birthday party. We knew that she was gravely ill, but it was the perfect occasion to get everyone together who knew and loved her. That day, she was all smiles and glowed with love, despite her deteriorating condition. We took a photo of Sarah with her husband that day, which we treasure. Her smile in the photo is infectious as it has always been and shines with love.

Sarah had a tremendous love for dogs, which started thanks to her husband. It didn't take long for Sarah and her husband to become an advocate for pet rights, as they lost their beloved dog Shadow to the bullet of a crazed landowner. Sarah and her husband pushed for pets to be recognized in the state of Vermont as companions, not just "empty animals" or property. Dogs are family. Anyone who has a dog understands that feeling. Our dogs are our children. Sarah told the Vermont press, "It's so important for people to really recognize the relationship between the families and their companion animals."

On the day Sarah passed away, the Vermont Supreme Court issued a decision that acknowledged that dogs are more than just replaceable.

On that night we learned of Sarah's passing, our dogs could not get to sleep. They were very restless. After awhile, I finally put both of them on our bed. A 65-pound weimaraner takes up a lot of room! While on our bed, our weimaraner started looking at a corner of the bedroom. That's when I got my tell-tale headache that alerts me to the presence of a spirit or ghost. Our weimaraner just continued to stare at the corner of the room. I knew it was Sarah. She let me know that she was at peace. What I found interesting was that she contacted our dogs first.

After they saw and likely heard her, our dogs would not sleep on their beds and had to sleep on our full-sized bed.

This is a good example of dogs' heightened abilities that humans don't share. Spirits are energy, and they communicate at a higher frequency range than humans can hear, although dogs can hear it.

We miss Sarah so much, but we know that she's now at peace on the other side with her loving dog Shadow. We're just glad that she let us know. This is Sarah, to whom this book is dedicated.

Examples of Spirit Animals Giving Messages

My Puppy Returns

In my first book, *Ghosts and Spirits: Insights from a Medium*, I devoted an entire chapter to my beloved weimaraner puppy, Buzz Wyatt, born on July 29, 2004, and tragically killed by a speeding car on February 22, 2005. He was six months old when his leash opened during a walk.

After his passing, Buzz gave me many signs that he is still around me, from musical signs to popping the lid off a trash can at the vet hospital where I took him for cremation. Buzz continues to let me know that he's still by my side through signs he's given me and others through the years.

Buzz's Birthday Visit to Another Medium

As I discussed in Chapter 8: Spirits, Anniversary Dates and Holidays, pets can use birthdays or anniversaries to give messages and prove it is they who are coming through. Thursday, July 29, 2010, would have been my puppy Buzz Wyatt's 6th birthday, and it marked a recent visit from his spirit. Buzz was a puppy when he was tragically killed.

Buzz has come back to me many times and has also made himself known to friends and our dogs Dolly and Franklin. We have his ashes in the house, and we feel him around.

At 5:30 p.m. EDT on July 29, our friend and learned medium Barb Mallon called me. She said that she had been driving earlier today and thinking about me when a dog appeared to have run in front of her car, in a gangly (clumsy) fashion, and as she went to slam on the brakes, the dog vanished! She said she knew it was Buzz and verified that when she got home and checked Facebook for my post about how that day (July 29) would have been Buzz's sixth birthday.

(PHOTO: Buzz Wyatt in December 2004. Credit: R. Gutro)

His feet were too big for him, so he tended to walk in a somewhat clumsy fashion. Barb's phone call of Buzz's appearance to her made my day.

Here's an excerpt from Barb's later email to me: *Oh, and after reading your book, I KNOW that was Buzz who FLEW by me! LOL! Holyyy ****! So cute! Barb*

Buzz Appears in a Photo

Although I've only seen Buzz materialize once in full-body form (and thought it was our weimaraner, Dolly), I hadn't seen him appear as an orb in pictures.

On March 17, 2010, we were taking photos of our dogs, Dolly and Franklin. We took two photos in a row, and to our surprise, it appeared that our late puppy Buzz also wanted to get in the photo. The first photo showed an orb to Dolly's right side. That's where Buzz's spirit decided to sit for the photo. An orb is a ball of light and is the most simple form of ghost or spirit energy as I discussed in Chapter 1: The Basics, What are Orbs?

A second photo, taken immediately afterward, confirmed that the rounded area of light with a colorful design in the middle was not a smudge on the camera lens, as it wasn't there.

Buzz's ashes sit in the very room where the photos were taken. The same holds true for anyone who has ashes of their pets or humans. Spirits are drawn back to their physical ashes from time to time.

Buzz Gives an Important Sign on Vacation

I mentioned that Buzz gave me a sign of his presence in 2010 by appearing to our friend and medium Barb Mallon.

On February, 22, 2011, Buzz gave another sign that he was still around. This time, we were vacationing in Puerto Rico, and it was during the week of his passing. I wasn't thinking of the anniversary date of his passing because I had instead decided to focus on his birth date. Buzz had other ideas, however.

While in Puerto Rico that day, we decided to walk in a certain direction in the Condado area of San Juan. As we were walking, we came across a dog walker with a pack of dogs. The first dog we noticed was a blue weimaraner. We were captivated by the dog's beauty, and I took a photo of the dog and the other 10 or so dogs in the pack.

After the dog walker departed, I suddenly received a message from Buzz. Buzz told me that he is still around. He said that he nudged me to go in that direction so we could run into the blue weimaraner. In fact, it was the only weimaraner we saw over our entire trip. There are no coincidences. Buzz led us in that direction so he could remind me that he's still watching over me.

A Dachshund's Spirit Says Hello

In the summer of 2010, my partner and I brought some groceries to a friend of mine who was home on bed rest. One month before, our friend's 14-year-old dachshund companion, "Rusty" had passed away. After entering his house and putting his groceries away, our friend took us through the house to show us improvements that were being done.

While standing in the main hallway and peering into the renovated bathroom, I was startled by a rustling sound right down the hall from where we were standing. It was little Rusty's spirit who came back to check in on his "dad," and Rusty was playing with a toy or some paper (like a newspaper).

I couldn't see Rusty, but I certainly heard him and immediately sensed him (I got my tell-tale headache in the back of my head). The noise he was making on the floor was about 10 feet from where I was standing!

It's a common occurrence for our pets to come back and keep us company from time to time once they've crossed over. It sounded like Rusty was playing with a toy on the other side. He wanted to let his "dad" know that he's happy, playing in the afterlife, and checking in from time to time. And whenever he checks in on his dad, he probably always brings a toy.

Holy Chihuahua: A Dog Comes to Me

In October 2010, we went to medium Barb Mallon's "double medium" event in Virginia and I got a couple of messages. One was very, very clear and it was from a dog. In fact, it was from a little Chihuahua.

The dog told me his name was "Chico" and he was connected with someone there.

As discussed previously, dogs do have the intelligence and personality to share messages. Dogs and horses have been recognized as having the intelligence of a 4 or 5-year-old human, while cats are estimated to have that of a 2 or 3 year old (Stanley Coren, author of *How Dogs Think*).

When Chico came to me, he showed me that he loved to burrow under blankets and sleep on chairs. That may sound pretty common, and it is, but he gave me his actual NAME. Further, he showed me that whoever he was connected to has a black or dark-colored dog (dogs can see blue, yellow and everything else in shades of gray or black). Chico said that he comes in from time to time and visits the black dog guiding its current master.

I wondered who this dog belonged to, but didn't get a chance to talk about him during Barb's event. So, after the event ended, I had a stack of my books that I was signing. (An article had just appeared in the *Washington Post* that day, October 30, so people knew who I was.) After one woman came up and bought a book, a second, younger woman started to walk up to me and Chico told me he was connected to her!

Before she even got to the table where I was standing I asked her if she knew a Chihuahua named "Chico" and she said, "Yes, that was my grandmother's dog that passed." I shared Chico's messages and she confirmed that she does indeed have a black dog. She left amazed that she just got a communication from beyond from a dog! I was just astounded that Chico actually directed me to the one person who he belonged to in the entire room of 50 people.

If you have a dog, cat, or horse who have passed, watch for signs. Signs are things like the sound of nails on the floor, objects moving, or a song on the radio that reminds you of them. They come back from time to time to say hello and remind you how much they love you.

Another Dog's Appearance

A friend from California told me about a night her late dog contacted her. On January 28, 2011, my friend Jill conveyed this story to me via email:

> *Hi Rob, Okay, a weird thing happened last night. About 12:30 am I got up from my daughter's bed to go to my room. As I was walking toward the foot of my bed there was a hazy image of my [late] dog, Quinn, lying on the floor. He never slept in my room, always between our doors in the hall. I tried walking around him, as he rolled to get out of my way. I could have been imagining it, as I was half asleep. But it seemed so real, I got into bed and my heart was racing and I couldn't stop thinking about it. Because I'm missing him is my mind playing tricks on me? Very bizarre. I just laid there thinking, I have to ask you!*

My response to Jill was:

> *Hi Jill - Not weird at all. Quinn was likely there. He knows that you're still grieving a lot and wanted to give you a sign that he's still around you. My puppy Buzz did that, too. He just wants you to know that you don't need to hurt so much, because he's still in the house with you. What a cool story. I love hearing stories about dogs and cats making appearances. It happens a lot more often than you think. Take comfort in it and talk to him this weekend when you're home. He can hear you.*

Audible and Date Signs From Pets

Our friend Merle loves cats. She lost her cat Seamus several years ago and told me that she hears "creaking" in the house whenever she senses that cat. Interestingly enough, Seamus also passed away on her late husband's birthday. That was a sign that Seamus and Merle's husband were together in the afterlife. (Remember, there are no coincidences.) Below is her email about her beloved cat that she lost and has given her signs of his return.

100

A Cat Returns

*Thu, 4 Mar 2010 - Hi Guys ~ I really enjoyed the section in
your book dealing with pets. I lost my Seamus {Shay-mus}
almost a year ago - overnight April 21/22, 2009. He was a
6 year old black cat with a few white hairs under his chin.
We got him to keep [my husband] Stan company and he
was always there to greet Stan when he'd come in from
dialysis. He'd sit on his lap - sleep beside us - and comfort
us whenever necessary. I really miss my kitty-kisses.*

*When Stan died {at home} Seamus checked him out. He
stayed there for about an hour. He was distant and
withdrawn for a couple of months, then started to go
through what I thought was abandonment issues. He'd be
really angry with me if I left him for any length of time, and
developed a real attitude! After a time he started biting the
fur on his belly, leaving bare spots. He died about 3 weeks
after being diagnosed with a mass - probably cancer - in
his belly {probably the reason for pulling out his fur}. The
mass wasn't attached to anything, but was growing and
interfering with his appetite.*

*Seamus died on Stan's birthday... sometime during that
night. Stan's birthday was April 21st. I truly believe Seamus
went to be with 'Daddy' for his birthday. I miss them both
like crazy - and I'm looking for signs that Seamus is nearby.*

*When I asked you on the ship if you saw anything around
me I was actually thinking of my beloved cat.... I hear the
floor creaking now and then and it makes me think he's
walking into the room, but that's all I've noticed. Hey - this
is an old house - floors creak! I talk to both of them almost
daily... but get no answers! I wish I could know they're
both close by. I have so many stories.*

Hugs, Merle

Horses See Spirits, Too

During a book event, I caught the interest of a number of people when I mentioned dogs, cats, and horses can give signs to those they left behind. One gentleman who had moved from the African continent to the U.S. told me that in his homeland, it is widely known that horses can see Earth-bound ghosts and spirits.

Like dogs and cats, horses have the ability to sense spirits as well as come back as a spirit. In terms of sensing ghosts and spirits, dogs, cats, and horses all hear at higher frequency ranges (which digital recorders pick up, but humans don't hear at that level).

The gentleman in the audience said that African people know that when a horse sees a ghost or spirit, a person can look directly in their eyes and see the ghost that the horse is seeing!

Bird Signals from Beyond

Birds usually can't communicate from beyond unless they possess a higher intelligence and characteristics that enable them to give messages after they've passed. Parrots, however, can come back with messages.

Parrots imitate people all the time, and one parrot owned by a woman named Sherry in Maryland proved how much like a person he was by giving her messages from beyond. Sherry and her parrot were together for 30 years, longer than she lived with any human.

Sherry said that when the parrot was alive and the phone would ring, he would imitate the sound of the ringer. When her parrot passed he decided to let Sherry know that he was still with her. Sherry said, "one evening, I was sitting at home and the phone rang, but it sounded like my parrot imitating the phone and not the actual ring!" When she picked it up, there was no one there. She said that she thought she imagined it, but it happened a second time and her cat even looked at the phone. It wasn't the phone but the parrot's imitation of the phone ringing. Sherry said she still picked up the phone and no one was on the other end of the line. Her parrot was giving her a call from the afterlife.

CHAPTER 14: MESSAGES FROM FAMILY MEMBERS

If you've lost a loved one and keep wondering when they're going to come to you with a message it may be that there are no messages immediately needed. After someone passes, they usually do want to let their loved ones know that they're okay, but grief blocks messages. When a loved one dies, it's a good idea to contact a medium to get the messages that your loved ones want to communicate.

Spirits will usually come through with important messages around holidays, anniversaries, birthdays or when something is happening in the life of the person for whom they have a message. Be especially vigilant during those times. I have noticed that grandparents seem to come through often.

Spirits won't just come through with a message of "hello." It takes some effort and energy for them to come through. Spirits make attempts to communicate when there's something to tell the living or some way they can help. It's the same as a living person picking up the phone and making a call when they have news to share.

In July 2011 during one of medium Barb Mallon's "medium event" sessions where she hosts a group of people, the spirit of a woman's mother came through with a clear message of thanks to her daughter (in the audience). Barb said that the mother's spirit was very grateful for the care that the daughter took of her mother when she was in failing health and called her a "tiger." There were many personal things that the woman in the audience acknowledged as Barb conveyed more messages.

During Barb's reading I also received a vision from the woman's mother. At the end of the session I told the woman that whenever she is depressed, sad, or worn out, her mother is there standing behind and putting her hands on the woman's shoulders. Her mom's spirit "has her back." The image I saw was of the woman in the audience sitting on a bed with her head hung down, and her mother's spirit clearly standing behind her with hands on the daughter's shoulders.

Following are some special times and messages that relatives shared with me and with some others.

Providing Comfort in a Hospital

In October 2011, I received an email from a woman named Michelle, a friend of a friend. Michelle asked for clarity on some experiences she had during a time of extreme illness. As I sat and read her email, her great aunt and a friend of hers came through with very clear messages. As someone who is still developing my abilities, I am always thrilled when the person can validate the messages I receive, and this was a wonderful experience.

Following are the emails, edited and with names changed to provide anonymity.

To: Rob Gutro   From: Michelle   Date: 25 Oct 2011

Dear Rob, I am a friend of Sara's. She provided me with your contact information. It is very gracious and kind of both Sara (in inquiring on my behalf) and you (in agreeing to accept an e-mail from me) to "listen" to my story. I appreciate your willingness to attempt to use your gifts to provide clarity for me. It means more to me that you could likely ever know.

I was diagnosed with Leukemia in June 2009. I had NO symptoms and only discovered the illness during medical processing for a transfer that my husband and I anticipated taking out of the area where we lived. I entered the hospital on the day of the diagnosis where I agreed to take a chemotherapy treatment that is in clinical trial phases.

Frankly, at the time that I entered the hospital, I was told that there was little chance that I would live. The medical staff did ask me if I would participate in the trial treatment - and I figured that if I could not live, perhaps someone would benefit from my decision to take the trial therapy and so, I did.

The treatment was "rough" - and following treatment I contracted Fungal Pneumonia and almost died from that. I came through the treatment and the Pneumonia much to the amazement of the medical professionals.

I actually recall very little about the whole "event." I recall doctors and medical students in and out of my room, but given the state of my body and how ill I was, well - I think that I have disassociated with aspects of the whole event. I prayed as hard as I could and have ever prayed - I prayed for another chance at life and I thought about all the things that I would contribute to the world, to my family - to anyone that would have my contributions if only I could be granted another chance at life. Probably sounds odd - I pleaded to be given a chance to be born again - not so much in the religious context, but in the soul context - to be given a chance to be a better person.

Anyway, much to the amazement of all - especially those at the hospital - I made a full recovery and went back to work normally (only thing missing was my hair!). I have been blessed to truly become a different person - my family and body has healed and loves that were lost are now found with new depth. I am truly a new woman. I jokingly say that I got all new cells and a new soul! I continue to be closely monitored, but have moved with my hubby to Florida where I teach. I have/we have been amazingly blessed to go on with life.

Leading up to my diagnosis I "felt" something or someone around me. I experienced (seriously) lights turning on and off around me - smells - usually smoke and flowers - found that odd (it happened to my hubby too) and just the feeling that I was/we were not alone in the house that we were living in at the time. We had built that house 10 years before and NEVER experienced any such activity prior to about 6 months or so before I became ill.

105

The experiences caused me great stress and frankly, did not have a positive experience on me or my relationships - I felt anxious and grumpy - that's the person that I was in that house at that time before illness.

I have to say that I felt on-edge and was not necessarily kind. It was as though I WAS PICKING UP ON SOMETHING, but that's probably just my making an excuse for the behavior of the woman that I used to be.

As I moved through recovering from the illness in that same house - I still felt something around me, but after the hospital, it felt more strengthening to me - like I had energy that a person in my situation should not have...almost as though someone or something was carrying me - energizing me. I felt this in and out of the hospital and the doctors routinely commented on how well I was doing and my energy level - I was always truthful with them stating that I did not know where the strength was coming from - and that's true - I didn't, but it actually felt to me like someone was holding me up and giving me a measure of supernatural strength.

The feeling of a presence would come and go during my recuperation - and slowly it faded...sort of faded away...it has been very gradual - I felt a final departure/separation from that energy only after having left and moved to another state. I would feel this presence especially with my daughter Maureen and at times when Maureen and I were socializing with a friend of ours who had actually lost her mother (Joyce) to cancer. Obviously, I wondered if the feelings that I had were picking up on Joyce, her mother (whom I never knew).

I cannot prove that there is or was anyone around me - but I felt it just as surely as if an individual was with me in the hospital and with me watching over me - literally giving me strength and lifting me up - I have no idea where the energy came from.

If you could - would you be willing to share any insight that you may have? I have had the feeling that whoever it is or was did want me to know, but I was not "smart" enough to guess! My guess would be one of my grandmothers, but in that I felt the presence sometimes the strongest when with my daughter and this other young woman...perhaps not my grandmother.

Thank you for listening, my apologies for the novel and BLESS YOU for your willingness to listen. Michelle

From: Rob Gutro   To: Michelle   Sent: Oct 26, 2011.

Hi Michelle- Thanks for sharing your incredible story with me. Sometimes when I'm at the computer spirits come through to me- it happened as I was reading your letter!

There are a lot of things going on there. First, I will say that before I read your last 2 paragraphs I was getting a sense that it was your mother's mother (?) with you. Did her name begin with a "B" - I'm hearing Beatrice, Belinda-

I'm also seeing roses, and even smelling them. Did you smell scents during your recovery? The roses were likely from her. [EDITOR'S NOTE: it turned out that they were from Joyce, the neighbor who passed of cancer].

Is there some significance in five minutes past two o'clock? I'm seeing a clock with that time on it. -perhaps it was the time of your appointment when you went to Hopkins, or the time you came out of treatment, or left the hospital. I'm unsure. Spirits give me symbols and signs I can't interpret.

The woman around you is strong. She was there during your treatment. She's showing me that she watched you in your room when you were walking around in a white hospital gown with little dark spots, flowers or some kind of pattern on it. She was always there during your treatment.

She said that everyone goes through trials here on earth, and that your illness made you a better person, and made you see life as you should- a true gift. It was a way to change the way you viewed the world, and taught you to appreciate life and every little thing life brings, even the downs as well as the ups. Those downs are there to provide lessons to achieve the next step in the afterlife.

What's the significance of the black dog, with a patch of white on his chest? I see a black dog sitting with paws outstretched. Is this your dog? A relative or friend's dog? This dog knew what you were experiencing when you were ill, and could smell the illness. The dog gave you strength. Whew. The woman (your grandmother?) is gone now. WOW. I hope you can make some sense of these things.

What I've learned is that your illness was part of your "life lesson" to help you become a better person, and achieve the next step (there are various levels in the afterlife, and we all come back until we achieve perfection). You mentioned that you think you got a "new soul"- actually it was more like a soul enrichment.

As for the entity turning lights on and off before your treatment and the odors- Those are all ways that spirits (those who passed into the light, like your grandmother) or ghosts (earth-bound energies) communicate.

Sometimes Spirits (positive energy) cause more irritation trying to send messages, by causing anxiety- so they tend to back off until they're really needed. Perhaps it was her way of trying to warn you about the illness- and the need for medical help. Ghosts (Earth bound) are negative energy and cause anxiety also, but because you're in a new house, there wouldn't be a ghost there unless it's tied to the land (or buried underneath it) - which isn't very likely.

Please let me know if any of these things make sense to you. Sincerely, Rob

To: Rob Gutro From: Michelle   Date: 26 Oct 2011

Hi Rob, I am so grateful to you for taking the time to respond to me.

Aha! That must be my great aunt (grandmother's sister and my mother's god-mother) Beverly. I have a photo of her with my grandmother that I cherish! She is the only "B" name in our family. I thought of her as a grandmother because she and my grandmother were sisters and they were always together - grew old together and lived just minutes from each other. I used to see her when we visited our relatives in the Midwest on summer vacations. That validation is very powerful to me because both my grandmother and Aunt Beverly were comforting to me as a child, they were from the "old country" farming women - very welcoming and "homey." They called everyone "honey" and you always felt like you were special around them...they were always about the children, cooking delicious meals etc!

I believe that I was discharged from the hospital around 2:00 p.m. - 2:05 p.m. - yes, somewhere in there. I recall that because I frequently take note of times on clocks! I have been doing that for years - and I am drawn to clocks at the same time over and over again! I wanted to note the time that I left the hospital because I remember thinking that I was 'born again' - all new cells and considered myself so blessed to have the opportunity to leave, in an environment where so many never got to leave.

I believe that the woman around me is "related" to the black dog. That very strong woman / presence could be Joyce- who would be the mother of the neighbor girl that I took care of. Joyce died of cancer. I never knew her, her daughter actually moved near us after her mother died. I am aware that she was a school principal and a very strong woman, active and well known in the community. My daughter and I included her in all of our outings - we knew she was lost without her mother - and tried to comfort her.

The daughter has a black lab with a white area on her chest...the dog is "Andi"...and my daughter LOVES that dog...both of our daughters love that dog. We used to dog-sit for the family...and that dog did have a special connection to us - she is such fun and always made us laugh. So, the dog would be the dog of the daughter of the lady that passed of cancer that I never knew.

Roses were Joyce's favorite flower - her daughter told me that when she actually brought me pink roses for Mother's Day...I thought that was very sweet of the girl because it put me in the same "category" as her mother and I felt honored...and I was working so hard at the time to try to comfort this young lady...not trying to be her mother, but trying to comfort her as a 'mom friend.' Additionally, I smelled roses in the hospital in the very scenario involving the hospital gown that you mentioned!

That gown was significant because during chemo they made me wear a gown because patients are so physically ill during treatment...the rest of the time I insisted on "street clothes," but during treatment they brought me this awful gown white with black dots on it...which I equated to being ill. I was a difficult patient refusing to wear a gown any more than I "had to."

Yes, a soul enrichment - I am me, but truly a different me and there is NOTHING - even the not so good - that I do not appreciate! It's odd - but true - I appreciate the bad days almost as much as the good days! I get the lesson that I was to have learned and I am not happy to have put my husband, daughter and friends through that experience, but I am grateful to have learned from the experience to the extent that I did. WOW - I just do not know what to say and yet I am going on and on! You have provided clarity and assurance that I am not "nuts"...seriously, I felt them and now I know that they were with me.

Many blessings and grateful appreciation to you Rob - Thank you from the bottom of my heart. Michelle

From: Rob Gutro To: Michelle Sent: Oct 27, 2011

Michelle - I'm so glad I was able to provide some comfort and assurance that you are being watched over and cared for from the other side. It amazes me when I get messages like these. Thank you for validating and understanding the messages. It's important for you to know that you're supported and loved by those on the other side at all times.

I'm glad you were able to identify your great aunt Beverly, and it makes perfect sense, given how loving she is. We all maintain our personalities after we pass.

Spirits will provide symbols like the clock to show that they were right there with you. Beverly was there with you as you left the hospital. She was there all the time during your stay - identifying the gown is confirmation of that. (I thought all hospital gowns were one drab color with no patterns, but that wasn't what she showed me!).

I think that it may have been Joyce coming through to me with Beverly because of the roses and her dog. Oftentimes there will be more than one spirit with someone in a hospital, but it's hard for me to identify all of them, so once I get a name, I usually attribute the messages to that one spirit. It's kind of like being in a room with people and I only hear the loudest voices. Although I didn't hear Joyce's name - she was the one telling me about her black lab, Andi, and providing the scent of roses to you.

Feel free to call me if you have any other questions. I'm sending you a hug from Beverly and Joyce. Rob

To: Rob Gutro From: Michelle   Sent: Oct 27, 2011

Hi Rob, I would be honored if you would include my story in your book.

111

My wish for you is that your authoring of such encouraging and reassuring publications provides peace for those of us who (thus far) are surviving, and the families of those who must say good-bye (for now) to those crossing over.

To be able to share such rich experiences in support of the pain of loss on this side is an amazing contribution to humanity and I am grateful to contribute a story that may bring peace and comfort (via you) to someone else out there so that when times get tough, we remember the provision of the creator in having provided us with help from the other side. Many Blessings and Thank You! Michelle

A Grandfatherly Hospital Visit

A friend in Indiana had a dream about her grandfather which appeared to be happening in real-time. Spirits who have crossed over can appear in our dreams (while Earth-bound ghosts cannot). Following is the story of Brandy's encounter when she was in the hospital expecting to deliver twins:

I had a dream that my grandfather was following me around and telling me the twins were going to be okay when I was in the hospital waiting for them to be born...it made me and my husband feel good knowing he is a spirit and at peace!

EDITOR'S NOTE: Spirits communicate to most of us through dreams. That's when our logical mind (that blocks them out) is asleep. Many times when people are in the hospital either expecting to give birth or slowly failing, they will receive messages from loved ones who have passed.

A Grandmother Visits

Susan is a friend of mine who lives in the western U.S. Following is what she shared about her encounter with her grandmother's spirit:

I wanted to tell you about my experiences following my Grandmother's death a few years ago. This is without a doubt, the most profound experience I ever had.

My Grandmother Ramsey was living with my parents in Colorado Springs at the time of her passing. Two days prior to her passing, she was admitted into a Hospice Facility for pain relief. I arrived the day before her passing and spent most of the next day with her until her death at approximately 12:34 a.m. on Halloween night. My sister, Kathy and I were at her bedside when she passed over.

The remainder of the night, I slept in my Grandmother's bed at my parent's house. Shortly after turning off the light, the portable humidifier at the foot of the bed began vibrating and making a loud racket which was followed by the metal louvered closet doors trying to open repeatedly against my suitcase which was preventing the doors from opening. After awhile, things quieted down and I slept.

When I told my mother of the night's occurrence, she said, "It was probably your Grandmother trying to get her dress out of the closet. She had one picked out for her burial."

My parents left for the funeral in Virginia leaving my brother, Don and I to watch over the house. Don and I stayed up until around midnight that evening, talking. Don was staying in the guest room in the basement and I was sleeping in my Grandmother's room on the second floor. Around midnight, I went upstairs to get ready for bed. While in the bathroom I began hearing what sounded like my Grandmother speaking to me. It sounded like it could be coming from the heating vent on the floor next to my feet. She said, "Susan, Susan I'm here."

113

In the background, I could hear many voices, music of some sort along with other sounds that were undistinguishable.

Not understanding what was happening, I immediately thought it must be my brother playing a trick on me. We had been talking about ghost stories before we went to get ready for bed. I then heard my Grandmother call out, "Not YOU!" I then distinctly heard my deceased Grandfather's laughter and what sounded like my Grandmother being picked up in a bear hug and swung around in a circle while she was saying, "whoaaa!" Then a very deep loud, echoing laughter started up and kept getting louder. It wasn't my Grandfather's laughter and sounded a bit scary. I quickly finished my business, stepped out of the bathroom and yelled down the stairs to my brother, "That isn't funny!"

I went directly to bed. Strangely enough I completely forgot about this incident the next day until a similar incident happened the next evening while preparing for bed. While sitting on the edge of the bed, I heard my Grandmother's voice. She seemed to be outside the open bedroom door saying, "Susan, Susan?"

I suddenly remembered what happened the previous evening and began to realize that my brother Don probably wasn't behind this.

Again, I called down the stairs, "I don't appreciate this!" I didn't get an answer and ran down to the basement. Don was sleeping in his bed behind two closed doors and never heard me calling down to him. I must have turned as white as a sheet and was extremely mad at myself for not realizing this was my Grandmother trying to communicate to me from the other side.

Don and I attempted to talk with her, but we never received another verbal response. The next day, she showed herself to me as a shadow walking across the upstairs landing. There was nobody else in the house at the time.

114

I now realize I was given the gift of hearing my Grandparent's reunite in the afterlife. I have no doubt life continues after we pass on thanks to my Grandmother!

EDITOR'S NOTE: Susan's grandmother obviously has a very strong spirit and was somewhat feisty. It takes a lot of energy to rattle a closet door. It also takes a lot of energy to create an audible noise. I find several things fascinating but not surprising. One is that the encounters happened in her bedroom. That's where she was most comfortable. Spirits always tend to come to where they were comfortable (my mother heard her mother's voice also when she was in a bedroom). Second, Susan was in/near a bathroom. Bathrooms have water, and water is a conduit for spirits to channel energies.

Grandmother's Spirit Visits Immediately After Passing

Our friend Merle experienced a visit from her grandmother immediately after she passed in May 1984. Following is Merle's story:

The weekend of May 4-6, 1984, I went to Ottawa, Ontario to visit my 96 year-old Grandmother Thomas. Her health was failing and she was ready to go. During the last years of her life her eyesight had deteriorated so she couldn't watch TV, knit, sew, or even read her Bible - all the things she had enjoyed throughout her life.

(PHOTO: Grandma Thomas. Credit: Merle)

I am her eldest granddaughter, and realized she'd want to see me, although she didn't know I was coming for a visit.

My aunt (her daughter) took me into the room where she was resting, and said there was someone here to see her. I could hear her saying: "It's Merle, isn't it? Merle has come to say good-bye!" Although she couldn't see me, she knew I was there.

She said she was ready for whatever God planned for her at this stage and was looking forward to seeing her Tom (my grandfather), and 2 children who had pre-deceased her one of them being my Dad. I couldn't stay long, because she was very tired and told me she didn't have much energy for our visit, but she was happy I had come.

Back home - Tuesday, May 8, 1984 - a workday. The sun was shining in my bedroom window and I was about to get up and get ready for work. My husband, Stan was asleep beside me. Suddenly something attracted my attention to the foot of the bed on my side. My Grandmother was there! I could see just her head and shoulders {she was always a short woman, but if the rest of here was there, I couldn't see it}. Non-verbally, she communicated that she had come to say good-bye. I tried to ask her what she meant, she just gradually faded from my sight. Out loud, I pleaded with her to stay a while longer, but she didn't - or couldn't.

I shook my husband waking him up! "Did you see that?" He of course had seen nothing, so I related the experience. It seemed like it had lasted quite some time, but in telling the story to Stan I realized it had all happened in seconds.

Eventually, I got up and got ready for work. Stan was at home recuperating from a hospital procedure. About 10:00 a.m. he called me at work and told me to sit down. My Aunt had called to tell me that my Grandmother had passed away early that morning.

There was no way I was going to get any more work done that day! I went home. Thank goodness I had told Stan about it earlier, because if I tried to tell him of my early morning experience after the fact, it would have sounded a little far-fetched.

116

We were back in Ottawa for her funeral on Friday - Mother's Day weekend. While there I spoke to my younger cousin, telling her "Granny came to say good-bye to me the morning of her death." Her reply was a little surprising but comforting: ""She came to say good-bye to all of us." I was too emotional to discuss it with her then, but it's something I need to discuss with my cousins, and see what else they can tell me about this amazing experience.

EDITOR'S NOTE: Often when a person passes away, their spirit will come to those they are close to, to let them know and to say goodbye as mentioned in Chapter 10: Slow Death Experiences, Funeral Homes, Wakes.

A Military Father Visits During a Show

In November 2012, we went to see Lisa Williams, an amazing medium. We noticed a group of six women in the row in front of us, all of whom came together. I got my tell-tale headache indicating a spirit was present and had a message for one of them.

One of the women was quite older than the other five, and I assumed her to be a mother of some or all of them. Sitting to her left was a younger woman (about 35) with dark hair who was clearly upset and kept crying into Kleenex. I was drawn to her.

The spirit was a tall, well-built man. He showed me that he was wearing "fatigues" something I associate with any branch of the military. He stood behind the 35-year-old woman through most of the show. He was sad and had so much emotion that it choked me up. He said he wanted the young woman to stop smoking (she later showed me a pack of cigarettes in her purse).

At the end of the show, I stopped her and asked her about the man. She said that her father just passed on October 19. She and her sisters were had hoped he would come through. I gave her the messages. Her dad was in the Air Force. I also explained how his showing me fatigues may not directly represent "Air Force" but simply military, which is how I associate with armed services of any branch.

She asked if I'm a medium, and I told her that I get messages when I get them. She also mentioned that her mother, who was with her, was skeptical. Regardless, it was one of the most moving experiences that night was the message I received from this man who wanted to let his daughter(s) know he was still around and loved them very much.

A Unique Message: A Wife's Love Knot

Love is the common thread that brings spirits back to us. Love is a knot that cannot be undone. Love is also the main emotion that powers spirits (those who have crossed into the light) to come back and give messages to those they left behind. In August 2010, I was at an event called "Karmafest," and heard interesting story from a man and his daughter about unique signs from his late wife.

As the man and his daughter approached me, I sensed the spirit of a woman was around them. He asked me about my book, and I explained that I wrote it based on my developing abilities to talk to ghosts and spirits. He asked about his wife who passed, and I instantly knew it was her around them.

His wife (who passed from an illness) immediately filled me up with so much emotion and love, it caused me to visibly shake. She wanted them to know that she's around them all the time.

I asked if either of them had received any messages from her. The man confirmed that some "odd things" happen around the house. He mentioned the strings from shades that he constantly finds wrapped in knots in the spare room (whenever he goes in there). He said that he and his wife shared a memory about knots, something from a movie they watched together. He said he couldn't understand how the knots kept happening, when neither he nor his daughter tied them and there was no one else in the house.

Obviously, it was a clear sign from his wife. The love that the man and his daughter have for his late wife is giving her the power to tie those knots.

118

Grandma in the Gym

On Thursday, August 5, 2010, we went to a local gym to work out. I mentioned to a young woman at the check-in counter that I wrote the book *Ghosts and Spirits: Insights from a Medium*, and she asked me several questions about the entities. After a brief conversation, we began to exercise.

While on the treadmill, I received a vision of a "grandmother-like figure" with grey hair pulled back in a bun and wearing a red dress. I also got a message about a young man with one earring. Upon leaving, I talked with the woman behind the counter about these messages, and she confirmed that it was her great-grandmother and that the last time she saw her alive, the great-grandmother was, in fact, wearing a red dress. The message was that she's around the young woman and watching over her. Spirits can communicate anywhere... and do!

Spirits Helping the Living Today

Spirits come back to provide helpful messages to the living when they need them. The following stories are incredible signs that my late grandmother and father provided to comfort my elderly mother. The things that they shared with me continue to surprise me as well.

Grandmother Helps Daughter Travel

Before Christmas 2010, I had a visit from my grandmother, my mother's mother. What's interesting is that she died years before I was born and I had never had contact with her before. I did see her in the light at the cemetery where my dad was being interred in August 2008. She was with my grandfather and others (including three dogs).

My grandmother appeared to me and told me to tell my mother (who is afraid to fly) that she would be with her on her trip to visit me. My grandmother told me to ask my mother to find the yellow knitted shawl she made for my mother, and she told me that my mother needs to wear a piece of my grandmother's jewelry.

I don't know of anything that my mother's mother had ever knit - only crocheted tablecloths - and certainly not anything yellow. When I called my mom, she immediately remembered something yellow and knitted from her mother which was stored in her hope chest! She found it and took it with her on her holiday visit (via airplane). She also found a piece of jewelry that was her mother's and wore that around her neck.

My grandmother's assurance of watching over my mother was enough to convince my mother to fly by herself. It was amazing. Having the ability to communicate with spirits is an incredible gift, and it allowed my mother to have the courage to travel by herself.

Husband's Spirit Guides Wife Find Something

On February 2, 2010, my father's spirit helped my mother find something she misplaced. That day I called my mom to check in with her and she told me the following:

> I have been looking for the back plate to the replacement kitchen wall phone for a couple of months now, and today your father led me to it. What's strange is that I found it on a chair right next to the microwave oven in the downstairs kitchen. I use that microwave almost daily and I know it wasn't there before.
>
> For some reason I asked your father to help me find that missing part of the phone today. I felt an urge to go downstairs, so I did. I happened to walk over to the microwave and was surprised to see that sitting on a chair right next to the microwave, was the missing piece of the phone! I can't believe I had not seen it over the last several months!

What happened here is an apport! My dad's spirit moved the missing phone piece to a place where my mother always looks. I had a similar experience when I asked my dad to help me find something and I found myself standing in the garage. It was there I found it, too, which was odd, because it had nothing to do with the garage.

120

My mother also mentioned that the light in her hallway continues to flicker whenever she walks by it, and she said, "I know that it's your father." It is.

Husband's Spirit Helps Wife Fly Home

In the previous section, I mentioned that my mother is afraid to fly. She did visit in April 2010 when she was accompanied on the flight down by my brother. However, he had to depart early, and my mother needed to fly home alone. But she wasn't alone.

On Sunday, May 9, 2010, my mother's two-week visit ended and I took her to the airport. This was the first time that she had to fly alone in her life and she was understandably nervous. When you're dealing with someone who is prone to anxiety attacks, sometimes news like "you'll be flying home alone" shouldn't be shared well in advance because that person will obsess over it. So we told my mother at the airport on the morning of her return flight after getting her through security (I got a special "non passenger escort" pass that let me take her to the gate (Southwest Airlines is wonderful!).

While we were in the security line, my mother saw a dime on the floor but couldn't pick it up. Spirits often toss pennies, dimes, and quarters in front of us to let us know they're there. Mom didn't tell me about it, and we went through security.

On the other side, she went to the restroom and came out holding a dime! She said "this dime was just on the counter in the restroom," and she explained about the other dime she had seen. She said "I know it's your father." She was right. I already had the tell-tale headache that lets me know a spirit or ghost is around. I sensed my dad sitting right beside her with his hand on her shoulder. I told her he was there to sit with her on the flight.

My dad told me to tell mom that she should return for Christmas, so I told her. She said "Like heck I will!" I heard my dad's spirit laughing and he said, "That's my Norma!" He stayed with us, and he showed me that he'd be sitting with her on the flight to keep her calm. She understood and was calmed and relieved!

When it came time for her to pre-board, I asked the attendant to take her to a seat and he did. Great service on Southwest! I didn't feel my dad's spirit with me and knew he had "boarded" the plane with my mother, so she was safe and sound. Once again, my dad came through from beyond!

Father Gives a Christmas Present Two Years After He Passed

During Christmas 2010, I got a special treat from my dad who passed in August 2008, there is no such thing as a coincidence.

My mother flew down to celebrate Christmas with us that year and stayed for a week. During her visit she gave me a brand new wallet she found in my dad's desk. She asked me if I would like to have it (I immediately accepted!). She said that she just "happened" to find it before Christmas. I know that she didn't happen to find it. It's obvious to me that my Dad guided my mother to his old desk and into that drawer where the wallet was located.

It was brand new, still in the packaging and had the price tag on it. My dad used to give gifts at Christmas and forget to remove the tags, so it was even more obvious it was from him! Thanks, Dad!

A Grandfather's Vision

On January 30, 2010, when I was talking on the phone with my mother, she told me something about my grandfather that I had never heard before.

In 2009 my mother told me about my grandfather's encounter with an apparition that became a solid form. This time she told me that her father (my grandfather) went down into the basement of their three-decker home (they lived on one level) in the 1930s and saw a bright light in one corner.

She said that when her father looked at the light and focused on it, it took the appearance of the Virgin Mary. Sometimes people who are extremely religious will claim to have been visited by religious figures. Usually when people have after-death experiences, they tell others that they had seen Jesus or other holy people.

My mom doesn't know how long the apparition lingered in front of her father. Because my grandfather passed in 1976, I have no way of asking why the apparition may have appeared to him at that time.

A Barber Brother Visits

Bob in Maryland told me that his brother was a barber. Shortly after his brother passed away, Bob was awakened three nights in a row with a feeling as if his hair were being combed. He said that he heard his brother as if through telepathy say that he was okay on the other side.

Spirits will provide us with easily identifiable signs from the other side. Such was the case with Bob's brother, who provided a sign through the profession he had while alive on Earth.

Our Loved Ones Watch Over Us

When our family members pass, they come back and influence decisions that will help us. They can help guide us and keep us from harm and give us a push to make decisions that will help us in some way.

In May 2010, my mother visited for a week. There was a last-minute decision to extend her trip another week that benefited both her and my younger brother. My brother has become her "go-to" guy (they both live in the same town) and as it turned out he needed some time to do some important things that week so he wouldn't be able to give my mom daily attention.

During the second week of her stay, I learned that a huge water main break occurred near the town she lives in, and it had cut off all drinking water for the week. I believe my dad influenced the last-minute decision to extend my mother's trip so she would be safe and hundreds of miles away from the water main break with plenty of water to drink and bathe in. Remember, there are no coincidences. Spirits have influence in our decisions.

CHAPTER 15: SPIRITS USE OF ELECTRICITY AND WATER ENERGY

Both Earth-bound ghosts and spirits who have crossed over are beings of energy from a life that previously existed. Because they are made of energy, they need energy to "power up." Think of a ghost and a spirit as a dim light bulb. When you add energy, the light bulb glows brighter, just as a ghost or spirit can gain strength and be in better "health" to give messages.

Some of the sources of energy that both ghosts and spirits use to manifest are electricity, water, heat, and emotional energy. The difference is that ghosts, who are essentially negative energy, feed off negative emotional energy such as fear, hatred, anger, and anxiety. That's why when you enter a house that you think is haunted, the ghosts are able to manifest by drawing power from your anxiety. Spirits, however, feed off positive emotional energy such as love, faith, hope.

Let's address electricity first. Ghosts and spirits can power up by electricity and can manipulate it. People who live in haunted places often report electrical disturbances such as lights going on and off. Telephones are another thing that ghosts and spirits use to convey messages. Ghosts are also known to drain batteries in technological equipment being used by ghost hunters, so they can gain power.

Water is another source of energy. If river runs through a town, you'll find a lot of haunted buildings. Ghosts or spirits can use water of any kind, including a shower, or if a ship is moving over the ocean. Movement of water provides energy. I've received a many messages from spirits while taking a shower.

Heat also provides energy to both ghosts and spirits. Heat is generated from fast moving matter (made up of atoms and molecules - groupings of atoms), and energy cause the atoms and molecules to always be in motion - either bumping into each other or vibrating back and forth. That motion of atoms and molecules creates heat. Ghost hunters often report "cold spots" when an entity is present. That's because the ghost is drawing the energy from the heat and slowing down the atoms, cooling the air.

Draining a Battery

Ghosts and spirits use energy in batteries to help them energize and manifest. According to electronics.howstuffworks.com, modern batteries use a variety of chemicals to power their reactions and create an electrical charge. Often during an investigation, just before a ghost manifests, moves something it drains batteries in a ghost hunter's electronic equipment. Spirits can also drain batteries to gain strength enough to give a sign of their presence.

Susan S.W. sent me an email that is a perfect example of how a spirit can drain a battery to convey a message.

She said that a year following her grandmother's death on Halloween night, Susan's watch stopped "at exactly the time of her death." She also said that she had recently replaced the battery prior to the day it stopped. I told Susan that it was not surprising because spirits can manipulate energy, and her grandmother likely drained the watch battery to make it stop on the time of her passing. The act was reassurance that she's okay in the afterlife and checking in on Susan from time to time. Her grandmother is obviously very connected to Susan. Susan mentioned that she saved the watch and it remains untouched to this day in her grandmother's jewelry box, which she inherited.

In 2010 during a ghost investigation in Baltimore, a ghost named William drained my camera battery when I was in the basement of a building searching for him. When I left the basement and returned to the first floor the camera went back on and regained a small charge. That meant that William's ghost had been draining the battery in the basement.

Telephoning from Beyond

There are many instances where spirits who have crossed use the telephone to contact the living and try to convey that they are safe and happy in the afterlife. In the book *Hello from Heaven*, authors Bill and Judy Guggenheim cite a number of stories where spirits called their loved ones and either spoke the living person's name, said they are happy and okay, or simply said hello.

Other times, the phone will ring and no one will be there, and no number or any read-out shows up on caller-ID. In those instances, some people have called the operator or tried the "star 69" to call back, only to get nothing. Spirits can manipulate electricity and telephones fit into that category.

A Telephone Call from Beyond

One Saturday, I was at the local post office mailing a couple of signed copies of my first book. The postal clerk asked me what was inside, and I told her. The topic piqued her interest. I told her the book is about my ability to communicate with ghosts and spirits and that I try to help others who are dealing with losses.

She told me that she has been trying to explain something that has been happening ever since one of her two closest girlfriends died. She said that when she and another close friend talk on the phone, they hear something like bells or chimes over the line; this has happened about ten times. It doesn't happen every time, and she said that she and her girlfriend both think that their mutual close friend who passed is trying to send them a message. I explained how spirits can manipulate electricity and make noises to send messages. Her late girlfriend certainly is trying to let them know that she's also on the phone.

The postal worker told me that she felt I was brought to her counter, and I agree. Her late girlfriend brought me there to affirm the messages of chimes on the phone. There is no such thing as a coincidence - spirits lead us to people and places at given times.

Sometimes spirits have even called people! When that happens, there is usually no one on the other end or sometimes the voice of the deceased person will be heard (if the spirit is strong enough).

Water Energy to Communicate

I've learned more about water and ghosts and spirits since writing my first book. I had the pleasure of taking a Caribbean cruise which allowed a number of spirits to come through to me. They used the energy created by the ship as it traveled through the water.

Messages in the Shower

I've received a number of messages while in the shower. This is not uncommon, because when people are taking a shower they relax, open their minds, and are usually at peace. Those are prime conditions for a spirit to be able to convey a message, and because they draw energy from the water.

A young woman from South America told me that soon after her boyfriend was killed, she often felt his presence while she was in the shower. She said that whenever she felt him, it was like she was being hugged. She also told me that in her homeland, it is a custom to place bowls of water around a room after someone in the family passes away to receive messages from them.

Messages on an Open Ocean

If you find yourself on a boat in open ocean, you're in a prime location for spirits to communicate. When the ship is moving through water, it's creating more energy. The following encounters happened while I was on a ship.

In February 2010 we took a cruise in the eastern Caribbean (and perfectly timed it to avoid record snowfall in the Mid-Atlantic). It was on a ship that was only two years old, so I was pretty sure there wouldn't be any ghosts on it. There weren't any ghosts, but there were spirits that tapped into me to give messages by using the water surrounding the ship.

Spirit in a Ship's Theater

During one of the evening shows, the spirit of a gentleman came to me, gave me his first and last name, and told me that he needed to tell Marjorie that he was around her and he was safe. Marjorie was possibly his widow and she was sitting somewhere in the audience. Of course, sitting in a crowded theater as a member of the audience made it impossible for me to identify who Marjorie was, so I regretfully couldn't pass along the message. That's one example of how no matter how important the message may be to the spirit, it is just not possible for a medium to get it to the intended person.

Spirit in a Ship's Cafeteria

A second spirit came to me while we were having lunch one day. The spirit of a man called to me telepathically several times. In fact, each time a certain woman walked by our table (which was about three times, as she kept getting up to get food and drink from the buffet), a man said, "My name is John." He told me he was connected to that woman.

John's spirit then showed me ivy, like the vine that grows up the sides of buildings, and I heard "like an Ivy League school." He said that the woman has a book of his that she inherited, that it has a dark cover, and to look where the bookmark was in it. After lunch, Tom convinced me to walk over and talk with the woman. It's always a little difficult to know who will think I'm crazy and who will understand. Fortunately, she was one of the latter.

It turned out that John was her late uncle. He used to go by "Jack," and he was an attorney that graduated from Georgetown University in Washington, D.C., not specifically an "Ivy League" school but one of very high caliber. She wasn't sure about the book, but made a note of it. The next day, she saw me and told me her uncle Jack was gay, but never came out of the closet (she apparently felt comfortable telling me that after seeing me with my partner). She said she thought that's why he felt comfortable coming to me.

Messages From a Mother's Spirit During a Show

The third spirit I encountered while on the cruise was an emotional one. We watched a "mind games" show and afterward were introduced to Bob Lawson, the mentalist and his partner. Bob did a handwriting analysis for us, and it was pretty spot on.

I suddenly sensed a lot of emotion around Bob's partner. While sitting next to him, I heard a couple of names that sounded like "Adelaide" but I wasn't certain. A woman's spirit was communicating with me. She showed me a cat, a color like green or aqua, and a white "house" or building. She filled me with so much emotion that I was physically shaking. Spirits will sometimes do that for mediums who are very sensitive.

Bob's partner told me that he had a very strong bond with his mother who passed, but her name was Margaret. Perhaps Margaret was trying to tell me about someone else in the family who had previously passed, and that she was with? That was a puzzle piece for Bob to decipher. Regardless, Bob told us that his mother's wishes for her services did not include having services in a church. Instead, she wanted the wake in a funeral home, and that's where it was. Apparently, she was very happy that they honored her wishes.

The cat belonged to Bob's partner's sister. It was a cat she got before her mother passed. I assume the mother loved the cat, too.

The final point was about the "color" that she showed me. It turned out to be more aqua or blue-green, and it was about a pen at the funeral home that mysteriously appeared. Bob said that when he and his partner went to the funeral home for his mother's services, there was no pen to sign the guest book. When they went looking for one and came back minutes later, there was a pen in the holder. The pen wrote in aqua-colored ink, unlike the black ink used on all the other entries in the book. They said that no one else came in behind them, so they didn't know where the pen came from. They thought it very strange that the pen appeared from nowhere.

The spirit of Bob's partner's mom was there to convey that she's around him. The message here is that if you are surrounded by water, or close to water, the energy in it enables a spirit or ghost to manifest and provide messages.

CHAPTER 16: LOCATIONS AND GHOST INVESTIGATIONS

Ghosts can be found wherever you travel in the world. Europe is famous for haunted castles and houses. Ghost stories have been handed down by word of mouth or published in Africa, Asia, Europe, North and South America, and Australia as well as island nations around the world. Even frigid Antarctica has had ghost stories from McMurdo Station on Ross Island.

This chapter includes ghostly encounters in California, Grand Turk Island in the Caribbean Sea, Maryland, Massachusetts, North Carolina, Pennsylvania and Puerto Rico.

Several of the encounters are from my investigations of historic properties with the Inspired Ghost Trackers of Odenton, Maryland. Others are from trips I've taken and some were submitted by others. I've listed them by state for easier reference.

CALIFORNIA

A Presence Attached to Hitler's Car in a Museum

EDITOR'S NOTE: The following story was shared with me, and it is a good example of how energies can attach themselves to objects. I've experienced this before, where energies were attached to a mattress or a piece of furniture. In this case, it's a car!

The Lyon Air Museum is located on the west side of John Wayne Airport in Orange County, California. It was founded by Major General William Lyon. In the museum you'll find authentic aircraft, rare vehicles, and related memorabilia, with emphasis on World War II.

The museum has a Mercedes that used to belong to Adolph Hitler. It was likely one of his staff cars. The outside of the car is in great shape, and the original leather interior is intact. There is a handhold on the roof over a side window. Hitler gripped that handhold when saluting to the crowd.

Once the car was obtained by General Lyon, his driver stood in the car, grabbed the handhold as to imitate Hitler's pose. He claimed a strange feeling overtook him that he couldn't explain and he got out of the car very quickly. No one is allowed inside the car now.

GRAND TURK ISLAND (Caribbean Sea): A Ghost in Coverely House

As I mentioned in a previous chapter, I encountered several spirits on a cruise to the eastern Caribbean. Several spirits on the ship were around some of the vacationers, but those weren't the only entities I sensed. I also encountered a ghost on an excursion on Grand Turk Island.

Grand Turk Island is an island in the Turks and Caicos Islands. There are about 4,000 residents, and the only current industry is tourism (so we were told). Former industries on the island include horses and sea salt mining.

During our visit we noticed the island was still recovering from Hurricane Ike's impact in 2008. On what appeared to be the island's main street, I encountered a ghost. The street housed a number of bed and breakfast establishments.

(PHOTO: The Coverely house with the one-armed ghost. Credit: R.Gutro)

I was drawn to what appeared to be an old ruined house surrounded by a lot of overgrowth. When we walked by the side of the house, I got my tell-tale headache that indicates there's a ghost or spirit present (the entity's energy overloads my head and gives me a headache). Just afterward, we found a plaque on a low wall surrounding the property. The plaque said that house is haunted by a one-armed ghost. It was the house of Alfred and Millicent Coverely, built in the 1830s, and was moved across the street to protect it from any storm surges created by hurricanes.

The plaque says, "Legend has it that an American couple who lived there after the Coverelys were greatly disturbed at night by the sound of footsteps dashing up and down the staircase. The second owners saw a small, plump white man with one arm. The former owner, Alfred Coverely, perfectly fit that description, as he only had one arm." So, it was Mr. Coverely who wanted to let me know that he's still living in his house, decades after he died.

MARYLAND

Many of the ghostly encounters in Maryland occurred during investigations with the Inspired Ghost Trackers of Odenton, Md. These are in alphabetical order by the city.

BALTIMORE: 3 Ghostly Visitors in a Bed & Breakfast

In 2010, I visited a beautiful bed and breakfast in downtown Baltimore and discovered at least three ghosts inside. The establishment shall remain nameless so that it is not affected by people who may be afraid of ghosts.

Upon entering the B&B I immediately got a dull headache in the back of my head, indicating ghosts were present. I sensed a woman on the first floor. The woman seemed to be a residual haunt, like a tape playing over and over, serving dinner in a dining room. There was a sense of peace and contentment. I felt that the energy did not have an awareness of the living people in the establishment.

There was a lot of energy on the main stairwell as I ascended to the second floor. When I arrived on the second floor, I went to the back room on the left side.

It was there that I encountered the ghost of a man who passed in that room. It seemed to be an intelligent haunt and one that may be responsible for making noise on the staircase when no one is around. As soon as I entered the room, the male ghost shared with me the sensations he experienced when he was dying, causing me to breathe heavily. Ghosts will sometimes share their pain of death with a medium to make their presence known. I have to ask them to stop sharing the pain and tell them I "get it."

Down the hallway on the second floor was a totally different energy. It was not one of anxiety and heaviness. Instead, it had a brilliant, calming, healing energy. I felt peaceful there, as if the ghost was a caretaker, loving and gentle. It was a total emotional opposite of the other room. One of the owners of the bed and breakfast told me that some guests staying in that "light" room felt peace and also sensed that someone was looking after them. It was a good feeling. Some ghosts are happy to remain behind like this one. This ghost was just content being there and taking care of guests in his room.

I learned that the bed and breakfast was once three different Baltimore row homes (all built in the 1800s), before they were merged into this beautiful property. Each of those entities I encountered was past resident of the homes.

BALTIMORE: A Ghost at The Book Escape

On October 23, 2010, I gave a talk and did a book signing event at The Book Escape in the Federal Hill neighborhood of Baltimore. Andrew, the book store's owner, was excited to have me make an appearance because Halloween was right around the corner.

The book store is located on Light Street and consists of two former homes that were built in the early 1800s. The two homes now form one complete book store with a nice courtyard in the middle of them.

When I walked through the front door, I immediately got a light headache in the back left side of my head indicating an entity (energy) in the building.

The woman who owns the building was also present, and she told me that the buildings were constructed in the early 1800s. There was also a tunnel underneath the right side of the building that had been filled in more than 100 years ago.

A reporter and videographer from the *Washington Post* came to the event. I had been speaking with them since February, and this was a good time for a piece in the paper, being close to Halloween. They interviewed me in the courtyard, and asked how I got my messages, when I learned of my abilities, and many more questions. It was a fun interview. I gave my talk to an intimate audience who all asked good questions.

Afterward, Margaret Ehrlich and Linda Furrow from the professional ghost hunters group "Inspired Ghost Trackers" of Odenton, Maryland, joined me. Margaret manages the group and uses scientific equipment. Linda is a medium. I had invited them because Andrew mentioned that there were some strange goings on in the two basements of the store, and he wanted me to investigate. There were two basements because the store was originally two old homes now joined together as one building.

Margaret brought a variety of scientific equipment including an EMF (electro-magnetic field) detector (to pick up electrical energy, which ghosts are made of), a thermometer to detect cold spots (as ghosts draw the heat energy out of the air so they can manifest), and a digital recorder, so we could ask questions to see if we got responses that were at too high a frequency to be heard by people.

We descended into the basement on the right side of the building, with the *Washington Post* reporter and videographer. Immediately, Linda and I were drawn to the back left corner and my headache intensified. I knew I was in the presence of a male ghost. I immediately felt unwelcome and said out loud, "There's a ghost in the back and I'm not going back there yet." The next day, I got confirmation that the entity in the bookstore didn't want me or anyone else in the basement.

The next day, Margaret emailed me a voiceprint that the digital recorder picked up when I felt unwelcome in the corner of the basement.

Margaret wrote, "This is in the first basement we went to and it was under the stairs. Rob and Linda were confirming with each other what they felt and this is what was recorded right before Rob said he wouldn't go back there. It sounds like a man's voice saying, 'Go away.'" When I heard the digital audio file, it was indeed a man's voice saying "Go away."

Now back to the investigation: Linda said "There's a man here. His name is William or Bill." I sensed he lived in the building when it was a house, and Linda confirmed that. I said "He's wearing a black suit with what looks like a string tie from the 1800s. He's telling me about the year 1837." Linda thought that was the year he passed. Linda asked me if the string tie is a ribbon and not a rope. I confirmed that it was a ribbon. She also "saw" him in her mind.

I sensed that the man was a lawyer, police officer, accountant or something that involved a lot of records. I kept seeing big books open which he was reading or working in, like a big ledger or legal book. Weeks later, when I learned who William was, I understood that the book was more of a log book.

In the corner where Linda and I first sensed William no orbs or mist appeared in photographs. There was nothing in the front of the basement and my headache faded. "William" was in the back of the basement, and Linda was still there reading him. We then returned to the first floor to get to the basement on the left side of the building. The two basements were original to the former houses and were separated by a concrete wall. The wall marked the separation of the structure when it was two homes.

Once back upstairs, a store employee explained that while sometimes looking for a book, he'd find the book mysteriously pulled out on the shelf. He said that one time a book actually fell off the shelf and onto the floor, and it was the book he was seeking for a customer! He said he thought that a ghost was helping him find these books and was not fearful of the entity.

He shared another event that happened when he and his girlfriend were painting one of the first floor walls red. His girlfriend watched her beverage slide 6-12 inches across the counter of the store, and no one was there!

135

That was a sign that the ghost may not have liked the color that they were painting "his house." Ghosts who dwell in their former home usually don't like changes made in the appearance of the home from the time they lived there.

(PHOTO: Officer William H. Callahan of the Baltimore Police Department and former resident on Light Street, Baltimore, Md.; Courtesy, Baltimore City/Craig Bencie Jr.)

We then descended into the other basement through a three-foot tall door that opened up into a regular-sized stairway. The group went into the basement while Linda continued investigating the first floor.

Officer William H. Callahan

I walked a few feet from the stairs and suddenly developed a severe headache. I said out loud "Ouch, I really need an extra-strength Tylenol!" I turned to my left and looked into a small area that was piled with boxes. I sensed that William's ghost followed us (he walked through the concrete wall that separated the other basement), and he was very close to me. I took multiple photos with my digital camera. When I came home I enlarged them on the computer and captured an orb (the simplest form a ghost can assume) in that corner. William was there (and apparently still unhappy that we were pestering him).

While Margaret had the digital voice recorder running, and I asked about 20 questions and heard a male voice mumble an answer.

What happened next is something that the videographer was able to catch on film. We watched the energy in my camera battery drain in seconds, the red outline of an empty battery flashed on the camera screen, and the camera went dead. William had drained all of the energy out of my battery (ghosts do that to get stronger to give messages)! He didn't want any more photos. The basement was his place, and we were apparently violating it.

After returning upstairs my headache faded and my camera suddenly came back on. William remained downstairs. Linda said William drained the battery because he didn't want his photo taken and it re-energized when I left his presence.

In the first floor bathroom there was a boarded up tunnel entrance. The old tunnel was used to bring slaves into the home from Baltimore harbor. The entrance had been covered up more than 100 years before. I sensed residual energy from the emotions of the slaves who passed through there.

William's ghost was the only intelligent haunt in The Book Escape, and he was not harmful. William found his place in the building and chooses to dwell in the basement while letting bookstore employees go about their business. Every now and then, William comes upstairs to help find a book or make his presence known. After all, the store was his former house.

Weeks after the investigation, my friend Craig was doing some historical research in Baltimore and discovered Officer William H. Callahan of the Baltimore City Police, occupied one of those two houses on Light Street, Baltimore, in the 1800s. That explained the feeling of the "law" that I sensed in William's presence, and the book was likely a police log book.

BALTIMORE: Entities On and Off the Mt. Vernon Ghost Tour

On September 25, 2010, I took the Mount Vernon Ghost Walk in Baltimore, and there were some active entities. Mount Vernon is Baltimore's cultural center, filled with interesting architecture and buildings that once housed Baltimore's leading citizens.

I met the ghost tour group in the "Owl Bar" of the Belvedere Hotel and immediately got a headache. There was definitely a ghost in the bar, but because it was so crowded there was too much emotional energy to be able to "tune into it." Think about being in a crowd of people and trying to listen to one person talking softly - that's how it felt to me while trying to "listen" to the ghost.

Once the tour left the bar, we then learned that there is a female ghost that haunts the bar and plays with glasses.

In September of 2011, I received a validation about my sensation in the bar. My friend and medium Ruth Larkin visited me from Massachusetts, and I took her to the Owl Bar, but didn't tell her what I experienced. She walked in the bar and looked around for a couple of minutes. When she came out of the bar she said "there's a female ghost in that bar."

Right after leaving the Owl Bar, Ruth said she saw the lobby as it appeared decorated in the early 1900s. She described seeing people walk through in period clothing, and large potted big ferns lining the lobby. As we continued to walk to the other side of the lobby, I looked at photos on the wall and there was a photo from the early 1900s that showed the lobby exactly as Ruth had described it!

Two other entities I encountered on the 2010 walk were not associated with the tour.

The first was an elderly woman's spirit who was with a woman in our tour group. The spirit kept calling the woman "cupcake." The woman was preoccupied with her husband or boyfriend, and this was one time I didn't feel comfortable relaying the message.

Later on the tour, another spirit (not a ghost) came to me as soon as a couple came out of a woman's club. The couple stopped to listen to the ghost tour guide. The spirit was a man named "Arthur" and belonged to the woman who just came out of the club. Arthur was watching over her and protecting her, like a father figure.

One of the places on the tour that is reputed to have ghosts is the Brass Elephant Restaurant. It has been closed for years and still sat empty in 2010. It is located at 924 North Charles Street, Baltimore, Maryland. The building was built in the early 1800s. At that time it was a home with a "hidden" fourth floor where servants lived. The restaurant is known to have many ghosts, and I did sense some energy in the building.

The tour guide implied that the reason the restaurant remains unoccupied is because of the ghosts. If you walk by the massive front windows, you'll see all of the tables are still covered with tablecloths and have centerpieces on them, as if the restaurant is just waiting to open. As of 2011, the only patrons are the ghosts that linger in the building.

BOWIE: Return to Belair Mansion - Little Anna's Ghost

On May 5, 2010, I returned to the Belair Mansion in Bowie, Maryland with my mother who was visiting from out of state.

The Belair Mansion (circa 1745) is a beautiful five-part Georgian plantation house formerly owned by Samuel Ogle, Provincial Governor of Maryland. Enlarged in 1914 by the New York architectural firm of Delano and Aldrich, the mansion was also the home of William Woodward, famous horseman in the first half of the 20th century. Restored to reflect its 250-year old legacy, the mansion is listed on the National Register of Historic Places.

(PHOTO: Anna Marie Ogle's nursery and bedroom in the Belair Mansion where her ghost still runs around and plays)

Several years ago, I took a candlelight Christmas tour through the mansion and sensed the ghost of a little girl in the nursery. A house historian later confirmed who the ghost was - little Anna Marie Ogle who died at the age of two in the mansion.

This time, my mom and I entered the mansion from the basement door, which is now the public entrance. We were met by a docent named Catherine who welcomed us. I immediately developed a headache in the back of my head, the tell-tale sign a ghost or spirit was present.

The docent showed us a 12-minute videotape about the history of the Belair Mansion and its many former owners, some of which include the breeders of two Triple Crown horse race winners.

We took a self-guided tour through the two upstairs levels of the house. On the first level, after passing through the dining room and moving toward the west wing (which was added in 1910), I felt Anna's ghost physically tugging on the right side of my shirt. I suddenly felt a cold spot on my lower right side as if a child's hand was placed above my waist, like a child trying to tug someone's shirt. I heard her ask me to "come upstairs and play with her toys."

We went upstairs and looked through all the rooms and came to the nursery where she passed. Anna kept giving me the feeling of a dry throat and a lot of swallowing. Then, I suddenly felt my body heat up and I started to perspire, as if I were sweating from a high fever. That was Anna sharing with how she felt when she had passed. Today, she's still at the mansion, still running through the house and trying to get any visitors that come by to play with her.

We exited the mansion and walked through the small garden, far into the backyard, where we saw the small fenced family cemetery. Amidst a number of other gravestones sits a tombstone with a crucifix on it, labeled "Anna Marie Ogle, 1849-1851."

HOLLYWOOD: A Disgruntled Ghost at Sotterly Plantation

Sotterly Plantation was built in 1703 on the shores of the Patuxent River in southern Maryland. In March 2011 I joined the Inspired Ghost Trackers group to investigate the house.

March is not a good month to be outside in Maryland, because the weather can be cold and winds can be biting. Such was the case on the day we visited this immense plantation of 100 acres. The plantation includes a frontier farm, and was once a tobacco plantation, a colonial port, and a landing for steamboats. Guided and self-guided tours can be taken through the mansion during different times of the year. For more information call 301-373-2280 or visit online at www.sotterley.org.

The house had gone through several owners, expansions and renovations, so there's always a chance one of the former owners who was really attached to the house could still be there.

We learned that James Bowles built the first two rooms of the house in 1703 and enlarged it in 1727. A later owner, George Plater III, expanded it again. Later the orientation of the house was changed by Dr. Walter Hanson Stone Briscoe. Finally, Herbert and Louisa Satterlee, daughter of J. Pierpont Morgan, restored the house to its current appearance in the early 20th century. Interestingly, the Satterlees traced their ancestry to Sotterley Hall in Great Britain, thus, the name of the plantation. The docent explained that the spelling of the name changed over time.

I wasn't expecting an entity in the house, as I didn't feel anything outside. However, I often don't feel an entity outside of a house. But just because a house is old, it doesn't mean there's an entity in it. Sometimes, energy in a house can be residual (from some emotional event that transpired in the past), and not necessarily an intelligent entity that can communicate.

We entered the oldest part of the house into one of the original two rooms. It was set up like a study and was furnished with a large desk and bookcase. After walking in, I got my tell-tale headache that told me there was an entity in the house. I felt a male presence in the room. With many prior owners, it was hard to figure out which one was still there, if it was even one of them. I needed another sign to help me figure out who he was. It didn't take long.

The tour guide then brought us into the "Women's Parlor." While standing there, I telepathically (the way I get a lot of my messages) heard a male voice say: "My house. I didn't invite you. Don't know you. Who are you?" I was uncomfortable because I knew I was not welcome in the house. The male entity was a commanding presence, like a military man, which I would soon confirm.

Immediately after I received that message, Ronda, one of the Inspired Ghost Trackers mentioned to me that she was feeling a pain in her neck, not a comfortable feeling. It was interesting that Ronda felt a physical pain while I received the verbal message.

Still standing in the parlor, I was suddenly drawn to the bookcase across the room and couldn't stop staring at a red hardbound book. I had to look at it for some reason. The book, written about J. Pierpont Morgan, was the only book in the case written by H.L. Satterlee - one of the owners of the house! Satterlee had pushed me to the book to let me know that he was the ghost that didn't want me or anyone in his home. I later learned that Satterlee researched his father-in-law, J.P. Morgan and would write and publish two versions of his biography: *The Life of J. Pierpont Morgan* (privately printed, 1937) and *J. Pierpont Morgan: An Intimate Portrait* (Macmillan, 1939).

Herbert Livingston Satterlee was a lawyer and author who served in the U.S. Navy as the Assistant Secretary from 1908 to 1909. That also explained the strong, commanding presence I felt.

We moved into the center of the house and I continued to feel that same unwelcome feeling and a lot of residual energies of slaves who lived on the plantation. The hallway door that now leads to what is known as the backyard, used to be called the front yard where people were received. It makes sense that slaves who were working in the house would open that doorway to greet people.

We were next guided into a large dining room. The atmosphere changed immediately and it was intensely peaceful. There were no energies there and no presence followed us into the room. Interestingly, the docent mentioned that that room was not one of the original rooms of the house and had been constructed later. After the dining room we were led through a small kitchen and outside into the backyard facing the river.

Margaret of the Inspired Ghost Trackers asked the docent if she ever had any ghostly experiences. The docent said that she did have one experience she couldn't explain. In 2010, she had walked down to the slave cabin (which was closed for the season when we were there) and saw a nicely set table inside. She said she returned to the mansion and asked the other docents who set the table, and everyone denied knowing about a set table. In fact, she said that the others said that there was no furniture in the slave cabins.

Our docent said that when she went back to the slave cabin to check, there was in fact no set table or furniture of any kind. She said she was certain she saw the set table but couldn't explain its disappearance.

Other claims included other employees hearing voices, singing, or crying, and witnessing lights turning on and off by themselves. Even smells of food and coffee have been acknowledged, when nothing was being served or prepared in the house.

Sotterley Plantation has at least one intelligent ghost haunting it in my opinion, that of G.A. Satterlee. There certainly may be more people who died and never left the plantation, too, but Mr. Satterlee was the only one who made himself known to me.

LAUREL: Montpelier Mansion and Double Medium Confirmations

On January 29, 2011 the Inspired Ghost Trackers group from Odenton, Maryland had organized tours of the Montpelier Mansion. Tom and I, and medium Troy Cline joined them.

The Montpelier Mansion is located on about 70 acres of parkland in Laurel, Md. It is operated and managed by the Maryland-National Capital Park and Planning Commission Department of Parks and Recreation (DPR), Prince George's County. The DPR learned that the house was constructed between 1781 and 1785.

Major Thomas Snowden and his wife Anne were the original owners. The house, located on a knoll above the Patuxent River, was built after Ann married Thomas in 1774. Both came from prominent Maryland families. They entertained the likes of George Washington and Abigail Adams in their home.

According to the DPR website (www.pgparks.com), the Montpelier Mansion, now a National Historic Landmark, is operated as both a house museum and rental facility. The DPR researched and furnished various rooms so they now look as they did at the end of the 18th century until 1830. Outside there is a garden and an 18th century summer house.

Upon entering the mansion, I got my tell-tale headache indicating that there is a ghost or spirit in the home. Tom reminded me that I sensed a woman in the home before in 2007.

We joined the Inspired Ghost Trackers and were ushered into a large room that originally used to be the kitchen of the house. Now, it is a large empty room with a fireplace on one side and many windows across from it. The walls in front of the windows were lined with chairs. We sat and listened to the tour guide, and the intensity of my headache increased tenfold. It actually hurt. That told me that either a ghost was next to me or there was more than one in the house. The latter turned out to be the case.

After hearing a brief history about the Snowdens, we walked down a hallway into the dining room. I was at the back of the group, and everyone had entered the dining room before me. As I entered the threshold, I felt as if I walked through a blanket of energy hanging in the doorway. I immediately got light-headed and dizzy. I stumbled back for a minute, then tried walking through again to experience the same dizziness. I told Ronda what had happened.

As soon as I entered the room, I sensed a man standing near the fireplace. He stood between five foot eight and six feet tall, and wore a dark or navy blue jacket and white shirt. He had dark curly hair and long sideburns. He didn't say anything to me, he just stood there. I couldn't figure out who he was or why he was there.

Once we left the dining room and moved a long hallway bordered by a front and back door, Troy arrived. Ronda told Troy to go into the dining room and check it out. Troy came back and said that he sensed a tall, slender man, about 6 feet tall with dark, curly hair. He said the man stood silently. Troy confirmed the same ghost I had just seen in the same place.

Later, I found a painting in another part of the house of one of the Snowden nephews. Mr. Snowden's picture and I was glancing back and forth between the two paintings. Troy approached me and said, "The man in the dining room looks like Snowden's nephew but not quite, right?" I said, "Exactly."

144

Troy then said, "The man in the dining room looked more like a combination of both Mr. Snowden and his nephew." I thought the exact same thing. This was another confirmation that both Troy and I saw the same man standing in the dining room. The man in the dining room was the first of two ghosts we would sense. The other was the woman that I sensed in 2007 and she was still there.

On the first floor, in a long hallway in the center of the house that connected the front and back doors, I sensed a woman standing by the back door. I told Tom and Ronda that there was a female ghost who used to open and close that door often and greet people as if they were getting out of horse-drawn carriages. I kept sensing horses on the other side of that door.

I asked the tour guide if there was a stable out that door. She said "There isn't now, but we believe there was, as this would be the way that horse-drawn carriages would bring visitors to the house." Another confirmation.

I then saw the woman ascending the staircase to the second floor. The group just happened to be going that way. So, once we reached the second floor we went into a child's bedroom and what appeared to be a child's play room. When we went into the back left bedroom, there was a sense of uneasiness in me. I was drawn to the back right corner (there was a chair there). I immediately sensed the ghost of the woman in that room. She "told" me that this was her room, and it's her private area. She didn't want others in this room.

She told me that when she was alive, she came in the room to dress and didn't even want her husband in the room. It didn't matter what her name was; she wanted everyone out. I later realized that this was the room where I felt hot and cold spots on my visit in 2007.

We left the room, and I pulled Troy aside. He immediately said that this was the female ghost's personal room, and she didn't want people in there. This was "her" room and was off-limits to visitors. Once again, Troy confirmed the messages that I also received. Troy and I were both picking up the same things.

145

Troy said the woman was wearing a blue dress and that she didn't seem to mind people in her home, but didn't want people to go in that room. Troy's sense of the woman's clothing was confirmed by Ronda of Inspired Ghost Trackers.

Once we left the room, Ronda told us about her previous experience in that room. She said, "I used to work the "Needle Art" show there every year around July. I would get there early before all of the people arrived, open the doors, turn on the lights, etc. One day while I was there alone waiting for the people to arrive, I was sitting in the breezeway (the one that goes between the house and the room with all the bookshelves), cross stitching, when out of the corner of my eye I could see the bottom of a dress. The dress was a robin's egg blue color and had a pattern kind of like herringbone. When I looked directly at the door where the person was standing, no one was there. This happened three different times, there was no doubt that there was a lady watching me sew."

Ronda described the woman's dress as "robin's egg blue." Troy also said that he saw the woman wearing a blue dress - proof that these two people saw the same ghostly woman at different times.

Troy emailed me later and said: "I remember sensing how gracious both ghosts were. With the exception of the upstairs bedroom, it was if they were both very proud of the place and happy to entertain guests. I loved the part where Rhonda asked me to check out the dining room. All she told me was that you had sensed a man with curly hair. It blew me away when I not only sensed him (immediately) but was able to verify his presence by comparing notes about his build and clothing with you! Troy."

After leaving that room, everyone descended the stairway and returned back to the large hall with the doors in the front and the back, and where I originally saw the woman 15 minutes before. Tom and I walked over to the back door (where the woman's ghost was), and Ronda joined us. All three of us realized that in one spot there was a cold sensation with a pulse! We put our hands in that same area and all felt the cold air and an energy that was pulsating.

146

The woman's ghost had come back downstairs with us and returned to the door. Both Ronda and Tom were amazed because neither had felt the sensation of a ghost before.

We left the mansion with a new awareness of the entities that still live there. A man and a woman, who may or may not be related and most likely don't even know each other, are still dwelling in the house. Ghosts are not always aware of other ghosts.

For some reason these two people never left the house even after death. They could have had unfinished business, the desire to stay back to comfort loved ones grieving over their deaths, or just love the house and never want to leave. Whatever the case, they lost their ability to know that they had to move into the light, and should be given the chance to cross over into the light.

RIVERDALE: A Woman and Child Haunting Riversdale Mansion

Riversdale is a mansion and a National Historic Landmark in Riverdale, Maryland. In February, 2011, we joined the Inspired Ghost Trackers for a private tour of the mansion because some docents there reported strange goings-on. I also encountered some strange goings-on and two ghosts that refused to leave the house they once lived in the 1800s.

According to the Prince George's County, Maryland Parks Department Web site for the Riversdale Mansion, (www.pgparks.com), it is a "restored, five-part, stucco-covered brick plantation home built between 1801 and 1807." The mansion is three floors and has a lot of decorative detail. The house was constructed by Henri Stier, a Flemish aristocrat. It was completed by Henri's daughter Rosalie and her husband George Calvert, grandson of the fifth Lord Baltimore.

The Web site for the Town of Riverdale Parks (www.ci.riverdale-park.md.us) noted that Henri Stier deeded Riversdale to George and Rosalie Calvert in 1804 and paid for the completion of the entrance hall, the central salon, and the dining room because the mansion was not yet finished.

The house was owned by several others after the Calverts moved out. The docent told us that the building was renovated with air conditioning and heat, and at one time was used as an office.

The ghost tracking group was led into a large room with portraits of the six Lords of Baltimore. Lords are similar to governors. Each of the portraits was about 4 feet high and 3 feet wide and were painted by Boris Luban, a Russian-American artist. George Calvert commissioned the six paintings in the 1940s, and they were hung in this large blue room which resembled a ballroom with a large chandelier hanging from the room's center. When I walked into the room, I thought that there was something odd about it.

I sat in a chair in the front left corner of the room to meditate and clear my mind. It was then that a ghostly woman appeared in my mind. She was in the room with us. She was in her 30s or 40s and had long, black hair and wore a large ruffled, almost hoop-like dress with lace on it. She was clearly the woman of the house; and I would later find out that she was Mrs. Rosalie Calvert. She was the wife of former owner and Baltimore Lord, George Calvert.

Rosalie gave me one strong message. She did not like the renovations that have taken place in her house (ghosts usually don't). She didn't like the carpet over her wooden floors or the air ducts in the walls that were not part of the house at the time she lived in it.

It turned out that the massive ballroom we were sitting in consisted of two rooms. The front part was a room with a large window facing the front lawn. The back part was a horse stable that was attached to the house. The back of the room was gutted and joined with the front part to form a massive ballroom.

I also got a name that had an "a" or "e" sound, like "Ella," "Eloise," or "Alicia," but not one of those names per se. There was a lot of energy and it was somewhat hard to focus in the ballroom. One thing I saw associated with the female name was a wooden rocking horse and a thin wooden chair. I would later learn that this was associated with one of the little girls who died in the house at 3 years old.

The girl who was communicating with me was Amelia, who lived from 1816 to 1820. Amelia showed me one of her favorite toys, although I didn't see a wooden rocking horse in the house.

I learned that most of the original furnishings of the family were missing, sold and not in the house, so Anna could have had a rocking horse. Later I learned Anna had eight siblings, five of whom reached adulthood.

I shared these messages with Margaret, and told her at the time that I didn't know who gave me the messages, but the sender, Amelia, became clear while touring the house.

Margaret took photos when I mentioned I sensed the presence of the ghostly young girl and adult woman. In one of the photos Margaret took, four orbs appeared, confirming that there was a presence in the room. In fact, there were two more ghosts in the room than I sensed. Because four of the children died at a young age in the house, the other orbs could have been those of her children. Apparently, I didn't sense the others because they were not as outspoken as the woman and the little girl.

(CAPTION: This photograph shows two orbs in the same room where both Rosalie and Amelia came to me. There were also two other orbs in the room. Credit: Margaret Ehrlich, Inspired Ghost Trackers, Maryland.)

After the docent finished his introduction, he led us into a first floor "office" that had wallpaper from the 1800s. One corner of the room had original wallpaper and showed a mural of people in a forest. The rest of the room was papered with a similar mural that was donated by a museum and was a close match. I happened to be standing near the corner of the original wallpaper when Rosalie gave me a physical sign of her presence and it startled me!

I was listening to the docent with my back toward the wall and no one standing behind me when I felt what was like a cold hand on the skin of my back (through my sweater and shirt)! It was on my back right shoulder, and I realized it was Rosalie trying to get me out of the room. It was unnerving to feel an actual cold hand on my back, as if it reached through my clothes and touched my skin!

As I moved into the hallway, the feeling disappeared. When I reached the main staircase in the hallway, Rosalie tapped me on the elbow, as I felt it go cold. She wanted me to keep moving. Apparently, there was something she wanted to show me upstairs.

The group ascended the stairs to the second floor. Once there, we proceeded to two small bedrooms (a boy's and girl's room) that faced each other down a small hallway off the main hallway. I suddenly got light-headed, so there was some energy there. The docent mentioned that children's laughter had been heard from these rooms by other employees.

We progressed down the main hallway to a big bedroom, which the docent called "the Henry Clay Room" because Clay had stayed in it at one time before 1850. I walked in and immediately tasted blood in my mouth. It was a copper-flavored taste, and I sensed someone died in that room.

We moved into the last bedroom at the end of the hallway. It was George and Rosalie Calvert's bedroom. It was a large room with a massive bed near the doorway. The bed had a large wooden frame with posts and a flowered canvas cover over it. I walked through the door and my heart pounded. I felt anxiety, death, and fever. There were many things very wrong in this room.

I heard Rosalie tell me, "This is my house and my room and I don't want you in it." One of the other members of the Inspired Ghost Trackers mentioned that she also felt anxiety. The docent told us that others previously sensed Rosalie in that room.

As we moved into the final room on the second floor, located next to the master bedroom, I got another message. It was about a leg injury. Suddenly, the inside of my right calf really ached. Ghosts and spirits will often share pain of death or injuries to get a message across and make themselves known. I asked the docent about a leg injury for Rosalie or George Calvert. He stated that when Rosalie was pregnant with one of the nine children, she fell off a horse and may have injured her leg. I later searched the Internet to confirm a leg injury but was unable to confirm it. I told Rosalie (in my thoughts) that she needed to cross over into the light and join her family.

That final room was actually a play area for the children and a place where Rosalie would sit with them. It was there that I saw a sign identifying the nine children and the ones who died at an early age. That sign mentioned Amelia, the little girl who came to me in the ballroom on the first floor. She wanted me to go upstairs to this room where her toy rocking horse must have been.

The tour group descended the stairs and viewed a couple of other rooms on the first floor, including a large open room with three large glass windows that faced the small backyard. To the left of the large open room was a dining room painted orange. As soon as I stepped through the door frame, my entire body had chills. Inside the room, on the left wall was a painting of a woman with long black hair looking at a 3-or-4 year old child. I knew the woman in the painting was Rosalie. It was how she appeared to me earlier in the ballroom. She must've been standing behind me to give me chills, or she walked through me.

After the docent's explanation, I felt Rosalie apparently walk through me as I was chilled up and down my entire body (I even had goose bumps). It was not a good feeling, and I was glad that the tour was ending. She obviously didn't want people in her house.

151

MASSACHUSETTS

BARNSTABLE: Ghost in Barnstable Restaurant and Tavern

In 2010, we took a trip to Cape Cod, Massachusetts to promote my first book. Before my talk at Cape Cod Community College, we dined at the Barnstable Restaurant and Tavern in Historic Barnstable Village. It's a beautiful restaurant with great food, excellent service and a ghost.

Upon entering, I got my tell-tale headache alerting me that there is an entity in the building. Then I felt a quick burning pain in my front right temple that disappeared quickly. During dinner I continued to feel the headache so I know the presence didn't leave. Derek Bartlett, manager of Cape Cod Paranormal Society, later told me the tavern is the first stop on his local haunted tour and that the ghost of a woman haunts it.

QUINCY: Residual Energy Around Josiah Quincy House

While visiting Quincy, Massachusetts in 2010, we stopped by the historic Josiah Quincy House (built in 1770). Quincy is actually pronounced "kwɪnzi," so if you don't say it that way, they'll know you're from somewhere else. Also, because it's in the Boston area, you need to not pronounce the letter "r" where it occurs and add it in where it doesn't belong. Then you're good to go!

The Josiah Quincy House was the "country home" of Revolutionary War soldier Colonel Josiah Quincy I, the first in a line of six impressive men also named Josiah Quincy, which included three Boston mayors and a president of Harvard University. Josiah number one inherited the land from his father and built his mansion on a 200-acre farm called the "Lower Farm." That farm was in the family since 1635.

The house has an unusual "monitor roof," the oldest known example of this roof style to survive from the original colonies. According to the National Park Service, "During the American Revolution, Quincy aided General George Washington by observing the British fleet in Boston Harbor from his attic windows."

The house is only open by appointment. While walking the grounds, I felt a lot of residual energy on one side of the house and saw vivid images of Colonial men, women, and children in period garb. I also saw images of horse-drawn carriages coming up to a door at the front of the home. Too bad we couldn't get inside.

QUINCY: Residual Haunt in President Adams' Home

During that same trip in 2010, we visited two other historic homes in Quincy. We did get tours inside the birthplaces of John Adams (second U.S. President) and John Quincy Adams (fifth U.S. President). The houses are side-by-side and still exist pretty much as they were when built in the late 1600s (by two families that owned them before the Adams family did). The two homes are part of the Adams National Historical Park, which is managed by the U.S. National Park Service.

During the tour of the older home, I didn't sense any intelligent haunts (that is, interactive ghosts), but I did feel residual energy in one room that turned out to be Abigail Adams' favorite room. I could sense her energy there and felt that it was "her favorite place." As I've mentioned before, whenever someone is very happy in a place, they can leave an emotional "footprint," and that's what Abigail Adams had done in one of the two homes.

NEW JERSEY

LAWRENCEVILLE: Revolutionary War Ghost in Action

The following story was submitted by a friend. He's had some experiences of his own and was kind enough to provide this story.

> *E.C said: I grew up in a single family rancher in Lawrenceville, New Jersey. The backyard has a scenic creek named Shabakunk that runs behind it, where I spent much of my childhood playing. My friends and I would often canoe down the creek with our dogs or play in the woods that surround it.*

I don't recall the first time I heard that there was a bloody Revolutionary War skirmish right on the creek where the house sits. Right after the Battle of Trenton, British troops stationed in Princeton were dispatched to engage General George Washington's troops at the City. They marched down the very same road that runs in front of the house today, a road that General Washington himself rode up and down many times, and it was at the Shabakunk Creek that they were met by American soldiers sent by General Washington.

I've been told by local historians that the skirmish was very bloody, and many soldiers from both sides were killed. Reportedly the creek turned crimson red from all the blood that was shed along the banks from the close contact fighting.

My friends and I would often imagine that there were dead soldiers buried somewhere in the creek banks or musket balls were lodged in nearby trees. On display in the local library is a small cannon ball that was found in a property nearby. I used to imagine that if I looked down long enough at my reflection in the creek, I would see an American or British soldier staring back up at me.

Our house has a basement with cedar wood paneling. Over the years many of my friends and relatives have said that they felt the basement was inhabited by a ghost or spirit.

I have felt the same - a presence of some sort, although I never saw anything that would suggest an actual haunting. But it does have a certain feeling; one often feels that one is not alone when in the basement. It was not until the last fifteen years or so that I became aware of two incidents that would appear to confirm this.

When my oldest niece Erika, who also lives in New Jersey, was very young, she fell down the stairs leading to the basement in her stroller. I recall hearing my sister screaming and running down the stairs after my niece.

Fortunately, my niece had landed upright and was fine. Many years later, she told me that when she landed at the base of the stairs, she looked up and saw a man floating towards her, with just his upper torso and head.

She said he was a younger looking man, with very dark hair, very pale skin, and that he was wearing "an old fashioned white shirt with a large ruffled collar." She said that he was looking at her intensely, but without malevolence; almost out of concern. She said that as he came closer, the cries of my sister and her thumping down the stairs drew the attention of the man, who looked up towards the stairs, and then disappeared just before my sister appeared. My niece retains this vivid recollection of the man to this day. She has never since had a similar ghostly experience.

Some years after hearing this story, my other niece Clare who lives outside New Orleans was visiting me. When I took her and her brother to lunch, she told me about her own ghostly experience in our house.

When she was around 12 years old, my mother was serving her breakfast in the kitchen. The kitchen has the door that connects to the stairs that lead to the basement; the same stairs that my oldest niece Erika had fallen down.

Clare said that my mom placed a plate with her breakfast on the glass table within reach of Clare. When Clare leaned over and reached out her hand to pull the plate over, the plate slid about one foot to her outstretched hand. I asked her "Clare, what did you do?" She replied in her southern accent "I said 'Grandma, someone just slid the plate towards me!'" I asked "What did Grandma say?" "She just said 'That's nice Clare.'"

My mom was not the most engaging conversationalist when preparing and serving food. I proceeded to tell Clare about Erika's experience. Clare had never heard the story, and she was surprised.

155

I asked Clare if she has ever had other ghostly experiences, and she replied "no." I also asked her if she felt scared, and she again said no, and that she did not feel that the ghost meant her harm.

Lastly, about five years ago, a childhood friend was over the house with his two youngest daughters, Summer and Kira. I used to joke to them about "the ghost" and they would always ask questions with incredulity and great interest.

For some reason, the light switch at the base of the stairs had been malfunctioning. It would not always turn on or turn off unless I toggled the switch back and forth several times. On a hunch, I told them about it, and said that perhaps the ghost was trying to communicate.

Excitedly, they followed me down the stairs to the light switch. I flicked the switch and it did not go on. I tried two or three more times and still, the light did not go on. I asked Kira to try, and on her first try, it went on. I tried to turn it off, and again, it would not go off. I asked Kira, and on her first try, it went off. We repeated this at least three or four more times, and each time, I was not able to either turn the light on or off, but each time, without fail, Kira was able to both turn on and off the light.

Prior to this, I used to wonder whether the ghost that my niece had seen was a solider or officer killed during the Revolutionary War Skirmish, and perhaps he had a young daughter or daughters that he missed dearly. I now believe that this remains a credible explanation, and that the ghost feels closest to those who remind him of the family he had to leave behind in service of his country. I still spend much time in the basement, from lifting weights to doing laundry. I often feel a presence, but never one that makes me fearful or apprehensive.

NORTH CAROLINA

ASHEVILLE: Ghostly Orbs at Thomas Wolfe House/Museum

During a visit to Asheville, North Carolina in 2011, we took the "Ghost and Haunt Tour" (Tel.: 828-355-5855). The tour guide, information about the buildings, and the ghost stories were great.

One of the stops on the ghost walk was author Thomas Wolfe's house. Thomas Wolfe was a famous author who immortalized his childhood home in the book *Look Homeward, Angel*.

We approached the Thomas Wolfe House from the north side, and I sensed something was peering at us from the second floor window in the front of the house.

As we rounded the corner and stood facing the front of house I snapped some photos of the second floor window where I sensed the entity. There were no orbs in the first couple of photos. An orb is the most simple form a ghost can take; once it obtains more energy; it can manifest into a human or animal shape (depending on what it is).

The third photo, which I used for the cover of this book, revealed a very obvious and colorful orb. Orbs usually have color and design in them, sometimes even faces can be seen in or around them. The orb was captured in front of the bedroom where Tom Wolfe's brother died. Our tour guide mentioned that Tom Wolfe's brother has been known to haunt that bedroom.

(PHOTO: Orb appears in third photo taken outside second floor bedroom, where Thomas Wolfe's brother died. Credit: R.Gutro)

The next day, we took a tour inside the house during the day, and I sensed a presence in the same bedroom. There were no other entities in the house, but there was a lot of residual energy on some of the furnishings, likely left over from the author himself. Information on the Thomas Wolfe House/Museum can be found at: www.wolfememorial.com/.

ASHEVILLE: Amazing Ghostly Orb at the L.B. Jackson Building

Another stop on the "Ghost and Haunt Tour" in Asheville was the L.B. Jackson building located at Pack Square. That's where I captured the most incredible orb ever on film.

Built in 1924, this building was the site of several suicides committed by jumping from upper floors according to our tour guide. One of the suicides was a businessman who jumped from the 12th floor during the stock market crash in 1929. Another suicide was that of a woman leaning out the 5th floor window.

I snapped four photos of the building with my FinePix A700 digital camera. Three of the four photos revealed nothing. The fourth photo in the series revealed a dark-blue-colored orb with what appears to be two eyes!

(PHOTO: Dark blue orb that appears to have two eyes, floating in front of the L.B. Jackson building. Credit: R.Gutro)

This orb was confirmation to me that those people who committed suicide from that building are still wandering around outside of the building where they died. The orbs prove that. After leaving the area of the building, we proceeded to the City Hall where I captured more orbs over an empty parking lot. We learned that where the parking lot now stands was once the location of a gallows for hanging criminals in the 1800s. Some of the ghosts of those people were still lingering at the site.

We also walked on a street lined with churches, where we caught photos of even more orbs. Several others were also getting photos of orbs on occasion with their digital cameras. The tour guide mentioned that this always happens when walking through Asheville.

PENNSYLVANIA

NEW HOPE: Dread and Anxiety in Haunted New Hope

On June 26, 2010, we decided to visit historic New Hope, Pennsylvania, after reading about it. It was a trip that I will never forget because of the intense energy and emotions that I experienced in the town.

As soon as we crossed the town line, I started feeling anxious, nervous, and miserable. It was like walking into a thick blanket of negative energy. It didn't help that the bed and breakfast where we were going to stay (but didn't) was full of negative energy. Of course, that was enough for me to cancel the reservation. Instead of making it a total loss, we walked through the town for two hours.

New Hope, Pennsylvania, runs along the west side of the Delaware River (yes, the one that George Washington crossed on December 25, 1776, and he did so just south of New Hope). As I've mentioned, running water near a town adds to ghostly activity.

This sensation was off the charts for me and I couldn't block it out. The tell-tale headache indicating ghosts or spirits hit me when we came into town. The negativity, the sadness, the fear, anxiety, nervousness I felt were making me really, really uncomfortable.

After returning home, I searched for reasons for the discomfort. Unsolved Mysteries.com said, "The New Hope area has been rumored to be haunted by a number of ghosts. So many, in fact, that it has been named "America's Most Haunted Town." Unsolved Mysteries.com said ghosts haunt: the Inn at Phillips Mill, Pickett House, Logan Inn, Odette's Restaurant, and the Van Sant Bridge. Each place has its own specific legend and witnesses to back them.

The Inn at Phillips Mill has a female ghost who wanders around, and another entity rocks in a rocking chair. The Logan Inn is reputed to have many ghosts. Room 6 is said to have three entities, a man in a mirror and two children. A Revolutionary War soldier wanders through the Inn, a girl haunts the parking lot, and an adult male lingers on the stairway to the basement.

The scent of a woman's perfume sometimes occurs at the Logan Inn and at the location formerly known as "River House." Unsolved mysteries.com noted a female ghost haunts River House and a deceased male artist haunts a house on Mechanic Street.

One of the places I felt the strongest energy was on the Van Sant Bridge. As I approached the bridge, I felt strong anxiety, sadness, fear, and nervousness that I couldn't understand. I knew that there were deaths associated with the bridge, but didn't find out what they were until I returned home.

Unsolvedmysteries.com said that the Van Sant Bridge is haunted by a woman and her infant. The young unwed mother was apparently thrown out of her house for giving birth without being married, and she jumped off the bridge to her death while holding her infant. The bridge is said to be haunted by her and her baby's ghosts. Local people say they sometimes hear an infant crying when there's no one around. But their ghosts are just two of several. Other ghosts who linger on the bridge are those of horse thieves who were hung from there during the Revolutionary War, and from time to time, are still seen hanging from it.

After researching the ghosts reputed to haunt the town, I felt it was no surprise I was overwhelmed with energy. The same thing has happened when I pass through a Civil War battlefield. Unfortunately, when we were in New Hope, I had not yet learned to tune out the energy, as I now have.

PUERTO RICO

San Juan: Energy and a Military Man at Fort Cristobal

In February 2011 we took a short vacation to San Juan, Puerto Rico. One of the places we visited was the Fort of San Cristobal.

On our way walking to the fort I saw a Spanish soldier standing in the woods, just off the sidewalk. He was wearing a metallic, silver, pointed helmet. The Spanish had arrived in Puerto Rico in 1493, and there were soldiers who resembled the one that I saw. I believe I saw a residual entity because it did not communicate with me.

In the 16th, 17th, and 18th centuries, Puerto Rico was a major military post during many wars between Spain and other European powers. It is centrally located in the Atlantic and became an important port between the U.S. and Spain. In 1898, during the Spanish–American War, Puerto Rico became a U.S. possession.

The fort is also called Castillo de San Cristóbal. The fort was finished in 1783 and covered about 27 acres of land, wrapping around San Juan city. Upon entering the fort, there is a small room where admission is paid and an entrance to a long, dimly lit tunnel that leads into the first floor of the fort. While walking the middle of the tunnel I felt as if I slammed into a wall of energy and residual emotion. It felt like a blanket. It wasn't an intelligent entity, but a lot of emotion from the soldiers that marched through that tunnel in preparation of defending the fort.

There was at least one intelligent ghost in the fort, however. It was a Colonel named Rafael who appeared to me on the top floor. Rafael said he was responsible for a group of men who manned the fort. He didn't give me any more information about himself, but he did give me information about the fort that surprised me.

After leaving the top floor of the fort, we walked through a couple of large rooms painted white. They looked like ammunitions storage rooms, however, I heard Rafael tell me that large rooms were used for bunking soldiers. I didn't know what to think.

About 20 minutes later we walked through another area with the same kind of rooms, and one of them was set up with wooden bunks on the left and right sides along the walls. The display showed that soldiers would sleep on those long wooden bunks. The wooden bunks had soldier's ammo bags, blankets, and what looked like rolls of fabric that acted as pillows. It was exactly what Rafael had told me the rooms looked like.

When I got home I did some research trying to find out more about Rafael. Ghosthunters-news.blogspot.com said: "Visitors to the park have seen strange apparitions and heard unexplained sounds." Some have encountered soldiers dressed in 18th century uniforms disappearing through the solid walls.

The most popular ghost story is about a guard house in the fort. The Garita del Diablo is a small guard house near an edge of the fort and isolated from the fort. Soldiers doing guard duty mysteriously disappeared. The story says the devil devoured their souls and bodies only leaving their uniforms and weapons behind.

While leaving the fort, I urged Rafael to move on into the light. He was no longer fighting a war and no longer needed to man the fort.

WASHINGTON, D.C.

Ford's Theatre: 3 Real Ghosts During "The Christmas Carol"

In December 2010, I saw a performance of "A Christmas Carol" at the Famous Ford's Theatre in Washington, D.C. Ford's Theatre was where John Wilkes Booth assassinated President Lincoln in 1865. I encountered three ghosts, and not the ghosts of Christmases past, present, and future. They were all very much ghosts of the past.

The National Park Service says Ford's Theatre was originally built in 1833 and used as a church. John Ford bought the building in 1861 and made it into a theater, changing its name. On April 14, 1865, just three days after General Lee surrendered at Appomattox Court House, President Lincoln was shot and killed while enjoying a performance with his wife Mary Todd Lincoln.

John Wilkes Booth and Two Later Confirmations

Before the show I was wandering around in the gift shop looking at items and trinkets when I sensed a presence next to me. It wasn't a living, breathing person. I was urged to pick up a "map" from the gift shop shelf, and when I looked at it, it read "Map of Booth's Escape Trail." A chill raced through my entire being as I realized the entity standing next to me was the ghost of John Wilkes Booth.

I "heard" him confirm and tell me that he is "John Wilkes Booth," and that he still returns to the theatre from time to time because it is the site of his "greatest act." He is apparently still atoning for his evil deeds and is trapped as an Earth-bound ghost.

Booth's ghost was confirmed in September 2011, when our friend and medium Ruth Larkin, joined us to visit Ford's Theatre.

Ruth discovered her ability of seeing spirits and receiving messages from a very early age. She tried unsuccessfully to suppress them and finally came to fully embracing her gifts as an adult. She is also a certified Reiki Master/Teacher and a Medical Intuitive. She can be reached at ruthlarkin10@gmail.com for readings in person or over the phone.

I didn't tell Ruth about my 2010 experience with John Wilkes Booth's ghost, and we walked into the gift shop and looked around. I started getting a headache at the back of the store and I felt cold. I then heard a man say, "Look up." It was not a request from a living person; it was from a ghost. I looked up and I was staring at a wall of books and other souvenirs about John Wilkes Booth.

Booth's ghost was talking to me, and I felt the temperature drop as he absorbed the energy of the warm air and left slower, colder air (molecules slow down, cooling the air when the energy is removed). Booth's ghost said, "I'm proud of my greatest act, killing President Lincoln." He was pleased the gift shop acknowledged his heinous act with books and other souvenirs. It was a confirmation of my experience the year before.

I told Ruthie to come over to me and she did. Her eyes grew wide and she said, "Rob, there's a really bad energy here. It's a man, and he was a horrible person, arrogant, headstrong." She said she didn't know who it was. I told her to look up at the souvenirs, and when she did, she gasped. "It's John Wilkes Booth," she said. Ruthie confirmed my experience.

We checked with the two clerks at the gift shop, who confirmed that lights turn on and off and the doors are unlocked from time to time. They told us that sometimes objects are moved, so they know that there's some entity in the gift shop - another confirmation.

Another confirmation of Booth's existence came two months later from another medium at the same production I first encountered Booth.

My friend and fellow medium Troy Cline went to see "A Christmas Carol" at the Ford's Theatre in December 2011, two months after medium Ruth Larkin confirmed John Wilkes Booth still lingered in the building. "A Christmas Carol" plays annually at the Ford's Theatre every Christmas. Troy said he sensed an "arrogant, hateful male presence in back of the gift shop." He sent me a text message at the time he was there.

I text messaged him back and said "look up from where you're standing and tell me what you see." His response was "John Wilkes Booth souvenirs." He immediately knew that he was also sensing John Wilkes Booth, just as Ruth and I had sensed him.

After my first experience with Booth's ghost, I did some research on Ford's Theater. I learned there are more than three ghosts there.

Paranormalknowledge.com said: The ghost of Abraham Lincoln and other ghosts have been seen at Ford's Theatre. Laughter, flickering lights and footsteps are also experienced in the theatre. People have heard the footsteps of John Wilkes Booth running to the presidential box, followed by the sound of a gunshot. Mrs. Lincoln's ghost has also been seen leaning over the balcony.

Cabinet.com said, "John Wilkes Booth is also believed to haunt the stage itself. According to several actors who have been involved in productions since, if they attempt to deliver their lines at a particular spot on left-center stage, they are overwhelmed with an icy sensation. Some even report becoming overly nauseous or begin shaking uncontrollably, often flubbing their lines in the process. At times, some even report seeing the ghost of Booth running across the stage in escape as he did so many years ago."

The Actress

In 2010, I sensed a second ghost inside the theatre. A female ghost told me her name was Marcia, Marsha, or Marcy. She showed me a dressing room backstage where she sat before a mirror. She had long, brown curly hair, and was dressed in an off-white lacy dress, with a high frilly collar. She was likely performing during the night of the President's assassination.

165

She said she was on the streets of Washington, D.C. and watched as President Lincoln's body was driven through the city on a horse-drawn dark carriage, with a black cloth draped over his coffin. I thought that odd because the coffins of Presidents are draped in the U.S. flag.

When I returned home later that evening, I checked for photos of Lincoln's funeral procession, and the coffin was covered by a black cloth and not a U.S. flag, just as Marcia showed me!

The Mysterious Man

The third ghost that tried to contact me in 2010 happened during the middle of the "Christmas Carol" production, so I couldn't concentrate on him. This was a male ghost (I didn't get a name or description). He came to me a couple of times during the production, and I finally had to ask him to leave, as I was trying to enjoy the show. Ford's Theatre is definitely haunted, and John Wilkes Booth is one of those entities.

President Lincoln's Summer Home

In 2011, I visited Lincoln's Summer Home, located in Washington, D.C. It was originally built as a summer home by George Washington Riggs. At the time this Gothic-Revival style cottage was built in 1842, it was located north of downtown Washington, D.C., and considered a getaway from the city. Now the city has grown and it lies in the middle of the District of Columbia. It sits 3 miles north of the Capitol.

In 1851, the U.S. government purchased the property to establish quarters for disabled war veterans. It still serves the same purpose today. The cottage is now called "President Lincoln's Cottage at the Soldiers' Home," because President Lincoln and his family lived there for a quarter of his presidency, during the Civil War from 1862 through 1864. According to the Web Site for the Soldier's Home, "The Lincoln family moved to President Lincoln's Cottage in June 1862 to escape the heat, congestion and noise of wartime Washington. They were also grieving the death of their young son Willie who had died in February 1862."

While touring the house, I got a dull headache in the back of my head, indicating that there was a ghost or spirit there. We entered the left-hand living room (where there is a fireplace) and I got stomach pains, indicating that there was a ghost there that was conveying to me how they passed. I couldn't tell if it was male or female. When I left that room the pain faded suggesting they died in that room. I didn't feel the ghost anywhere else in the house. Obviously the energy was attached to that room.

At the end of the tour, I asked the docent about anyone passing while living in the house. She mentioned that one of George Riggs' daughters had passed in the home, but couldn't tell me what she died from.

CHAPTER 17: STORIES FROM OTHERS

This chapter contains experiences from others. They were sent to me to show others different situations where ghosts and spirits appear, and to show that people who are not mediums have had paranormal encounters.

The Bedroom Ghost
Submitted by Susan W., Colorado

It wasn't until I turned forty that I began having paranormal experiences. At least, paranormal experiences that I recognized as such. I visited my sister, Kathy, during winter that year (1995) and stayed in her basement guest room. I was working night shift in a Skilled Nursing Facility at that time, so wasn't used to sleeping at night. I stayed awake all night and finally heard my brother-in-law, Bruce getting ready for work upstairs. This must have been between 4 and 5 a.m. It was still dark out. Suddenly I heard rustling as if fabric was rubbing together or as if someone was rolling on the bed. The bed covers began to get pulled off me as I was laying on my back and held on for dear life. I was able to keep the sheets from being pulled off.

While this was happening, my pillow began to be pulled up on both sides of my head and was being held tight by some unseen force. It was unseen because I was too afraid to open my eyes.:-) Needless to say, this really freaked me out! The entire experience lasted only a few minutes and when it ended, I jumped out of bed, ran to the bathroom and locked myself in until I heard my sister up in the kitchen. This entity didn't bother me for the remainder of my stay but I must say I really didn't get much sleep after that happened!

Kathy told me that several months after my experience an acquaintance of hers was being shown the house. When she got to that room, she refused to go in and left the house quickly and said there was something bad in that room.

A Ghost That Appeared to Children
Submitted by Susan W., Colorado

I had some paranormal experiences that I didn't recognize as paranormal when they were happening. When my siblings Don, Kathy, and I were in our teens, we were living at Plattsburgh Air Force Base in base housing.

I found out 30 years later that Kathy was being haunted by the voice of a man saying her name every time she went into the bathroom. I had no idea this was happening to her. When she told me 30 years later, I remembered 3 of my friends using the bathroom (at different times of course :-)) and telling me after leaving the bathroom that they heard a "deep voiced man" calling their name.

All of them asked me if my dad had been calling them from downstairs when they were in the bathroom. Of course, he was not. I never thought these were paranormal in nature. I thought they must be hearing somebody from outside calling another person with the same name. I was shocked when Kathy told me of her experiences in that apartment years later - especially when I recalled the same thing happening to my friends.

That same year, we had 3 little girls enter our apartment when no "living person" was home at the time. I was just getting home from school, walked in and heard children's voices upstairs in the bathroom. I ran up and found 3 and 5 year olds playing with my mother's lotion and makeup. When I confronted them and asked what they were doing there, they said the man told them to come in when they knocked on the door. When I asked where this man was, they said they hadn't seen him and had only heard him telling them to come in. They said they thought he was in one of the bedrooms down the hall. Of course, I checked and found no "man."

I didn't want the little girls to walk home alone as I felt they were too young to be wandering around the base by themselves. They lived a surprising distance from our apartment. I asked them how they ended up so far from their homes and why they decided to pick our apartment.

169

They couldn't think of a reason, but again said the man told them it was alright to go inside to play. When talking to the mother of one of the girls, she was surprised they had wandered off as far as they had and said that they had never done that before.

EDITOR'S NOTE: This story reinforces the idea that children can see ghosts and spirits easier than adults because their logical minds haven't developed.

Dreaming of Lost Loved Ones
Submitted by Merle M., Canada

Occasionally I dream of my late husband Stanley. For the first year I didn't and was becoming VERY frustrated! Our dear friend Val passed four months after Stan, and her husband David and I were experiencing severe withdrawal as neither of us dreamt of our spouses. I guess it was after my experience of sensing Stan in the room that I started to dream.

I've had only a few dreams - one warm & loving and others where he's 'there' but not really part of the dream, sort of in the background, and always as a younger man. David said he eventually dreamed also. He was very traumatized by Val's death - although she had cancer they both thought it was under control - he was devastated. As he came more and more to accept her passing, the dreams started.

However, I'd be remiss if I didn't share a very amazing 'dream'. I don't know if I was dreaming or not - but I became instantly alert! Early morning, 12 days after Stan died a vision came to me.... I hesitate to say an angel, but whatever 'she' was I saw a smiling face, large bright eyes and short curly blond hair. She leaned over me, looked right into my eyes and said "Stan's here - he's here". Wow!!! I took that to mean he was safe, and I hoped, at rest.... he had been so ill for so many years. Yet it was still some time before I started to dream of him. Do dreams of deceased loved ones always mean they are trying to contact us - letting us know they're close by? **EDITOR'S NOTE:** The answer is yes.

On page 21 of your book, "Ghosts and Spirits: Insights from a Medium," you say "Ectoplasm looks like a mist." That's exactly how I'd describe Stan's visit on the anniversary of his passing.... it was a WARM mist, like a cloud in the room, and when it dissipated the room felt cold. You would have loved the house we lived in for 20 years. We had a 'friendly' ghost there - the kids nicknamed him Casper. We all experienced many happenings and sightings. We believed it to be the ghost of the previous owner. His family sold the house moved away. I think he was lost.

EDITOR'S NOTE: Dreaming of Stanley (her late spouse) indicates that he's passed into the light. Sometimes it doesn't happen right away, because once a soul/entity leaves their physical body, they sometimes want to hang around and try and offer comfort. My dad stayed the entire week (we watched the electricity in my mom's house do strange things...it was dad) and didn't move into the light until the funeral.

As I mentioned in my first book, my dad also appeared to me as a younger man. So, Stanley's appearance as a younger man (younger than when he passed) makes sense. When we pass, we choose the appearance we want to take on, which is usually younger. When I saw my dad, he took on an appearance of when he was in his 30s.

I was happy to see that Merle's friend David dreamed of his late wife, too. She apparently stuck around him on Earth for awhile until he was able to accept her passing. Then she moved into the light, knowing he came to understand what happened to her. It was then that she was able to finally come to him in his dreams.

Dreams are the main way loved ones communicate to us, because it's the only time our logical mind is asleep. Our logical thinking blocks out our ability to recognize or trust signs from those who have passed. When we're asleep, our logical mind sleeps, too, enabling spirits to convey their messages.

A Mischievous Kitchen Ghost
Submitted by J.S., Maryland

There was a ghostly presence at my last residence that had a bad habit of turning on the burners on my stove - pissed me off to no end (and no - it wasn't a gas leak or something - the freaking knobs would be turned ON!) And I KNOW once I felt someone watching me and my skin just crawled - I remember RUNNING down the hall and literally diving under the covers! I'm just glad that entity didn't follow me to my current home!"

EDITOR'S NOTE: Ghosts or spirits do turn appliances on and off to get attention. One story involved a dishwasher that kept turning on the "pot scrubber" setting in Virginia. The person telling the story said his previous roommate (now passed) used to always use that setting. Clearly, the ghost wanted to let the homeowner know he was checking in from time to time.

Ghosts in a Former Hospital
Submitted from: Jennifer N., Maryland

I worked night shift for 7 years in an elder care facility. The building had originally been the county hospital about 100 years ago. Some of the elderly female residents I was assisting would tell me that they had delivered their children in this building when it was a hospital. While working there, many unexplainable things happened to me.

Strangely, I didn't experience any of the hauntings at the facility until after I had returned from a trip where I had my first paranormal experience. Once I had my first experience in this care facility, I had so many unexplainable things happen that I don't know where to start.

I think the first thing happened one sunny morning when I was just getting off work and heading out to the parking lot to get in my car. I was the only person in the parking lot - everyone else in the facility was busy getting residents ready for breakfast. As I approached my car I suddenly heard a woman crying loudly. She was crying as if something horrible had just happened.

I immediately started looking for this woman as I thought it might be a fellow nurse needing consoling or possibly a visitor very upset about something. I walked all around a large flowering bush from which the crying seemed to emanate but there was nobody there.

I began walking down the driveway beside the facility that led to morgue behind the building. The loud crying persisted throughout my walk to the back of the building. It was as loud as it was when I was next to my car in front of the building. It seemed to be following me. I could find no living person crying. The crying lady followed me back to my car never answering my questions as to who she was, what I could do to help her or why she was crying. I finally drove home and went to bed.

I experienced the crying lady two more times, both inside the building and on the wing closest to the driveway to the morgue. My assistants also heard her. We checked all of the rooms to no avail. None of the residents were crying, they were all fast asleep.

The cook had a similar experience when he was arriving to work early in the morning. It was still dark outside and he was the only person in the parking lot. He heard the crying lady behind the same bush where I had thought she must be.

He brought his flash light with him and pushed the bush back fully expecting to find a living person there. When he discovered no living person behind the bush he made his way back into the building as fast as he could.

EDITOR'S NOTE: It sounds like a woman at the facility may have perished outside and is still wandering around lost and panicked, and needs to be crossed over.

"Maggie's Ghost" Appearance
Submitted by Sam and Jem, Pennsylvania

Every Christmas my parents would take my sister and me to visit my paternal grandmother's family. They lived in a rather large house, very old. According to my great aunt it had been in their family since the Civil War.

I didn't really like visiting since I didn't really know them. I used to go to one of the sparsely used parts of the house to read a book alone.

One Christmas when I was 7 or 8 years old I was reading in one of the older rooms and a nice lady came in and sat down with me. The room was poorly lit, so I never saw her clearly. All I could see was that she wore an old fashioned dress and her hair was dark colored. When she sat next to me I became very cold. She said that I should put on my jacket, which appeared right next to me when I know it wasn't there before.

We talked for a long time. She was nice and very friendly. I got the sense that she was lonely like me. I told her about my best friend, Jem, and she remarked that he was a part of my soul, and I am part of his. She said that we should never let our friendship die. We had to stop talking when my mother called for me. I asked her name, and she told me it was "Maggie." I said that I was glad to have met her and found a new friend. She looked very happy, and I think there were tears in her eyes.

I never saw her again after that. When I questioned my relatives, they said that there was no one called Maggie in the house. Jem says that this was the first sign of my psychic abilities. We both agree with Maggie's assessment of our relationship.

EDITOR'S NOTE: I absolutely believe that she saw a ghost in the house a former resident. Obviously it was an "intelligent haunt" as the ghost was able to communicate with her and sense things about her and Jem. I wouldn't be surprised if she learns of a woman named Margaret or Maggie, who lived there. - It may be in records in City Hall.

As children, we have the ability to have open minds. Open minds are necessary to see and sense ghosts and spirits. As we grow older, we learn to be logical and lose the ability to be open-minded. We also tend to become more pessimistic, which also acts as a barrier to the senses.

The following is an example of a little girl that I met, who had a ghostly encounter:

Little Girl's Drawing of the Ghost in Her House

At a book signing I did in 2010, I met a woman and her 6-year-old daughter who told me of a female ghost in their home. The ghostly woman apparently died in the home. I asked the little girl to draw a picture of the woman she saw, and the little girl drew a woman in a long brown dress holding a flower basket. The girl's mother mentioned that a Mennonite family lived in the old house, and I believe that this woman was the mother of that family.

The little girl said that when she saw the female ghost, she hid her head in her hands. She told me that when she looked through her hands, the ghostly woman appeared to vanish through a wall. I told the little girl's mother that the ghost probably lived there before and loved the house so much that she didn't want to leave and move into the light. The ghostly woman had not harmed anyone, so she likely just wanted to continue living in her house and share it with the new family.

I instructed the little girl's mom to tell the ghost aloud that she doesn't live there anymore and that a new family now lives there. It's important that the ghost moves into the light and join her relatives. The mom agreed that the ghost was nothing to be afraid of, but it was a little unnerving to see things moved (apport).

Paranormal Experiences and Sensitivities
Submitted by Jennifer N., Maryland

I have been interested in ghosts and the paranormal as long as I can remember...back into the middle elementary school years.---in fact, when I was 10, I know I had already decided that being a 'ghost hunter' was one of the things I thought I'd want to 'be' when I grew up. I remember writing about it in a school assignment. I know that at the age of 8 or 9 my mother started to worry about me because I loved to read books about mythological monsters, werewolves, and ghosts.

I'm not sure what sparked my interest, but my stepfather (who has been in my life since the age of three) has had a lifelong career as a funeral director, at one time was the owner of three funeral homes, and even now in retirement is the general manager of a large cemetery. So, from a young age I was exposed to more talk about death than the average kid! I remember experiencing a feeling of panic as a little girl regarding aspects of death--- the inevitability of it, the 'foreverness' of it, and the awful possibility that there might be nothing on the other side.

I was raised in the Methodist church, so I was taught about heaven and hell, but I've always been a person who has wondered and questioned, even as a kid, and maybe not always out loud.

I think I am often pretty sensitive to the atmospheres of places; however, there have been three times that I can remember when things have happened to me that were definitely strange, seemed to have no logical explanation, and may have been paranormal.

When I was a teenager and young adult, I worked at a conference center in my hometown it was a large house built in 1732, on 80 acres of its original estate. This place was magical...a great place to work, with great people who were like a family. The house has a long history of ghost activity. It seems that nearly everyone who has worked there has had some kind of strange experience.

I worked in many departments during my 10 years, from housekeeping to management. I always felt safe and welcome, despite the fact that I very often felt I wasn't alone, when there wasn't another living person with me.

One evening when I was in college, during the time that I was working as a waitress, I was alone in the dining room after all the guests had finished eating, clearing the tables. The dining room was the house's original kitchen....large enough to seat about 30 people. There were two large windows on each of the east and west walls and a large original fireplace on the north wall. In the center hung a brass chandelier which I believe was original to the house.

The chef was cleaning the kitchen, and the other waitress was washing dishes. There was a closed door between me and the kitchen, and another closed door between the dining room and the rest of the house. I was busy clearing the tables, stacking dishes into a tub sitting on one of the chairs, when behind me I heard a 'thump' and turned around in time to see a large black olive --(yes, an olive....we would serve a dish of olives at each table during dinner, large black olives which still contained pits. As you can imagine there were often several left in the dish at the end of a meal.) -- falling from the direction of the wall, high up near the ceiling, as if someone had thrown it!

As I said, both doors were closed and I was alone...a wee bit shaken, I went into the kitchen to see what everyone was doing...both of my coworkers were absorbed in their tasks and clearly hadn't had time to sneak out, scare me, and race back to look casual.

There was nothing for me to do but go back to the dining room and finish my work, alone with that creepy feeling! I continued to clear tables. I was in the center of the room, directly under the old chandelier, when another olive fell from directly above me.....a direction where clearly no person could be! Now I was slightly alarmed and went back into the kitchen to tell everyone what had happened. I really was pretty excited that finally, the Ghost seemed to have made contact with me personally.

About 8 years later, I was married and the mother of a small child. My husband and I moved to a tiny town on the Eastern Shore, on the Chesapeake Bay, which had been a steamboat resort from about the turn of the century until about the 1950s. We lived (and still live) in a house originally built as a summer cottage. The second floor had two bedrooms opening onto the hall, which also had a door which connected the two rooms.

One room belonged to us, and the other to our little girl; we never used the connecting door, and in fact, we had furniture placed in front of it on one or both sides.

Occasionally, I would be sitting in the living room on the first floor, and hear very distinct footsteps moving above, from one bedroom to the next, all the way across the house....seeming to pass through the adjoining door. Other people sometimes heard these too, sometimes at the same time as me, and sometimes when they were alone. My mother heard it repeatedly, the night she stayed with my daughter when my husband and I were at the hospital waiting for our youngest daughter to be born.

We have neighbors whose house is only about 12-15 feet from ours and while we can hear noises from their house, they never sound as if they are coming from within our house, as these footsteps did. We haven't heard these steps for many years now---at least not since we converted the attic into a master bedroom, and the second floor rooms became rooms for our daughters. I don't really know anything about our house other than that it was built in 1930 by a man named Owens. He still has descendants in the area, one of whom has even done some work on our house. The land our house was built on was (in the 19th century or earlier) once a farm.

A Youngster's Energy

If you have the ability to tune in to ghosts and spirits, public places can be filled with messages from entities trying to communicate. During a book signing event in Annapolis in 2010, my friend Troy (also a medium) joined me and confirmed messages.

A young boy (about 7 or 8 years old) stopped by the book signing event with his older sister. The boy stopped right in front of the table where Troy and I were sitting and said, "Tell me about ghosts and your book." I found it odd and he stood stock still.

I explained what's in the book and asked if he had ever seen a ghost. He said no. However, he was visibly shaking (his sister said he was cold but it was summertime), and that energy hit me and the muscles in my sides started shaking. Troy looked at me, and I knew he was also reading it.

When I mentioned ghostly "orbs," his sister asked what that meant. The little boy stated, "It's a ball of spiritual energy." (It is!). He then asked if I could sign a promotional post card to him, which I did. He thanked me and left with his sister. After talking with Troy, we confirmed that the little boy was much more in tune with the energy of spirits and ghosts than he was admitting. He radiated light and emotional energy, and both Troy and I confirmed it.

The Mysterious Tall Man

Another person at that event that we found memorable was a tall, thin, older gentleman in a blue shirt. He walked past us twice. The second time, I could see there was a spirit attached to him, walking with him. I immediately turned and looked at Troy, who confirmed that he also felt a second, spiritual presence with the tall stranger.

CHAPTER 18: CONCLUSIONS

Since I wrote my first book, I've had many more encounters with both Earth-bound ghosts and spirits who have crossed into the light. I've learned a lot about what makes them stay or go.

Ghosts have taught me that they have become trapped here and need to cross over into the light. I've learned Earth-bound ghosts give off negative energy and power up by negative emotional energy as well as physical power sources. They also emit negative energy to the living and cause emotional problems for them. Some ghosts stay behind because they have regrets for things they did when alive and try to obtain forgiveness to cross over.

Spirits who have crossed into the light are full of life and love and draw from those emotions to make their presence known. Spirits have taught me that we must all treat each other well and not discriminate, hate, or separate. Everyone should have equal rights, and everyone should be treated as we expect to be treated. We need to help and love each other, even though sometimes that feels impossible because we're human.

Spirits have taught me that doing something to "get even" with someone or belittling someone to make yourself feel more "powerful," is only hurting yourself. Being mean to others could lead to your being trapped as an Earth-bound ghost, begging for forgiveness when the living person you hurt can't hear, see, or feel your cries for help and forgiveness. Other ghosts stay behind because of unfinished business, to help their family cope with their grief, or they don't know they're dead yet (sometimes after a sudden death it takes awhile for a soul to realize they physically died). Other souls may choose to continue dwelling in their former home after death because they've grown so attached to it.

Many ghosts cry for help. They want help to be freed from their earthly prison. Ghosts have conveyed that being an Earth-bound ghost is like being in a prison. It's like being in solitary confinement, where no one can hear you or help you (unless they're a medium). Imagine being kept away from your family (who crossed into the light) for an eternity.

Spirits and ghosts have conveyed to me that life and the afterlife is about how we treat each other. Try to be good or decent to everyone. Don't cut people off in traffic. Don't belittle each other, use someone or intentionally cause harm to another. Don't bully, tease or harass others either, as you will regret it, if not during your time on Earth, certainly after you pass. Keep in mind that trying to obtain forgiveness after death is a lot more difficult than trying to receive it while you're alive, because most people don't pick up on signals from ghosts and spirits.

Know that there is an afterlife. You can call it heaven or just becoming one with the universe.

Scientifically, energy cannot be destroyed, but it can be changed. The human soul (and the animal soul) is emotional energy, and our loved ones remain with us whenever we call to them, see a photograph of them or think about them. They come to us in our dreams (if they've passed into the light). They will be waiting for us when it is our time to pass, to welcome us into the next life. It is my experience that love never truly dies, and it even transcends from the afterlife to this life. Just keep an open mind, watch for signs, and have faith.

If you get messages from someone who has passed, they might be difficult to figure out. It doesn't mean what you're getting is wrong. It just means that spirits are showing you something that makes sense to them, but may not make sense to you or the person they're trying to communicate with. Sometimes, too, the person for whom the message is intended won't immediately understand the significance of what a medium has been shown. Regardless, we are all energy and we all need to treat each other well. I learned that from the living as well as the dead.

To follow along on my latest adventures, share your adventures or questions, on my blog at: ghostsandspiritsinsights.blogspot.com/. You can also email me at Rgutro@gmail.com, and follow me on Facebook at "GhostsandSpiritsInsights" and Twitter at "GhostMediumBook."

BIBLIOGRAPHY

CHAPTER 1: THE BASICS, What Are Orbs?
Ghosts on Film, by Troy Taylor, 2005, Whitechapel Productions Press.

CHAPTER 1: THE BASICS, Ghosts Need Help, Too
Helping Ghosts: A Guide to Understanding Lost Spirits, by Louis Charles, 2010, Angels & Ghosts, LLC dba Angels and Ghosts Publishing.

CHAPTER 2: ENERGY AND ENERGY BEINGS
Ghost Hunting, by Jason Hawes, Grant Wilson and Michael Jan Friedman, 2007, Pocket Books.

CHAPTER 3: RECEIVING SIGNALS
Hello From Heaven!, by Bill and Judy Guggenheim, 1997, Bantam Books.

CHAPTER 8: SPIRITS AND ANNIVERSARY DATES
Barb Mallon, Medium, Chantilly, Virginia, www.barbmallon.com

CHAPTER 11: WHAT ABOUT SUICIDES AND MURDERS
Barb Mallon, Medium, Chantilly, Virginia, www.barbmallon.com
Lisa Williams, Medium, http://www.lisawilliamsmedium.com/

CHAPTER 12: COMMUNICATIONS FROM NON-SPEAKERS
Barb Mallon, Medium, Chantilly, Virginia, www.barbmallon.com
Soul Survivor, by Bruce and Andrea Leninger, 2010, Grand Central Publishing.

CHAPTER 13: SOME INSIGHTS ON ANIMALS
Ghost Dogs of the South, by Randy Russell and Janet Barnett., 2001, published by John F. Blair publishing.
Inside of a Dog, by Alexandra Horowitz, 2009, published by Scribner, a division of Simon and Shuster.
How Dogs Think, by Dr. Stanley Coren, 2004, published by Free Press, a division of Simon and Shuster.

CHAPTER 16: LOCATIONS AND GHOST INVESTIGATIONS

MARYLAND

www.Fellspointghost.com

www.Sotterly.org

www.Pgcountyparks.com/places/eleganthistoric/Montpelier_intro.html

www.Pgcountyparks.com/places/eleganthistoric/riversdale_intro.html

ci.riverdalte-park-md.us/history/nineteenth.html

NORTH CAROLINA

Ghost and Haunt Tours, Tel. 828-355-5855

Thomas Wolfe House, www.wolfememorial.com

PENNSYLVANIA

www.unsolvedmysteries.com/usm464955.html

PUERTO RICO

ghost-hunters-news.blogspot.com/

WASHINGTON, D.C.

Ford's Theatre: Three Real Ghosts During "The Christmas Carol"

www.Paranormalknowledge.com - John Wilkes Booth

www.Cabinet.com - John Wilkes Booth

Medium Ruth Larkin, certified Reiki Master/Teacher and a Medical Intuitive. She can be reached at ruthlarkin10@gmail.com for readings in person or over the phone.

ABOUT THE AUTHOR

Rob considers himself an average guy, who just happens to be able to hear, feel, sense and communicate with Earth-bound ghosts and spirits who have passed on.

Rob worked as a radio broadcast meteorologist at the Weather Channel and was heard providing forecasts on more than 40 radio stations across the U.S. He worked for various other science and related organizations and has almost 20 years of on-air radio broadcasting experience.

Rob enjoys spending time with his partner and their dogs. He enjoys taking ghost walks in various cities and visiting historic houses and sites to see who is still lingering behind and encourages them to move into the light to find peace.

He loves to exercise, enjoys a good cup of coffee, paperback mysteries, talking about ghosts and spirits, weather, superheroes and still reads and collects comic books. In fact, since he was a boy, one of his favorite superheroes has always been the ghostly avenger created in the 1940s called "The Spectre."

Rob feels that the most rewarding thing about communicating with those who passed is to share messages with their loved ones left on Earth, to provide comfort that life goes on after our time on Earth, and that our loved ones are still with us.

If you have questions or stories you'd like to share please feel free to write me at Rgutro@gmail.com. The author's blog, Facebook and Twitter (GhostMediumInsights) is updated every week. The blog can be found at: http://ghostsandspiritsinsights.blogspot.com/.

16651952R00107

Made in the USA
Charleston, SC
04 January 2013